SANJEEV KAPOOR'S

COOKING FOR PREGNANT WOMEN

In association with Alyona Kapoor

Popular Prakashan

www.popularprakashan.com

Published by
POPULAR PRAKASHAN PVT. LTD.
301, Mahalaxmi Chambers
22, Bhulabhai Desai Road
Mumbai - 400 026
For KHANA KHAZANA PUBLICATIONS PVT. LTD.

First Published 2014

(4349)
ISBN: 978-81-7991-790-9

Nutritionist: Seema Goel
Design: Sameer Madye
Illustrations sourced from Shutterstock

Printed in India
by Sai Print 'o' Pack
New Delhi - 110 020

ACKNOWLEDGEMENT

Anjali Sawant
*
Anupa Das
*
Armaity Motafram
*
Bharati Anand
*
Harpal Singh Sokhi
*
Jaaie Jaiwant
*
Lata Lohana
*
Manish Purohit
*
Neena Murdeshwar
*
Nisha Dingra
*
Priyanka Bose
*
Rajeev Matta
*
Saurabh Mishra
*
Sheetal Kadam
*
Swapna Shinde
*
Urmil Kapoor
*
Vinitha Ramchandani

AUTHOR'S NOTE

Becoming a mother is perhaps the most fulfilling moment in the life of any woman. Giving birth to a healthy and happy baby is definitely something all to-be-mothers hope for.

Babies are completely dependent on their mothers to develop well – both physically and mentally. The maternal environment in which the foetus develops is vital to the health of the child in later life too. And to ensure that the baby develops in a conducive environment, as well as the birth weight of the child is optimum, one of the most important factors is good nutrition for the mother.

I may not be a doctor but I am aware that a woman has to prepare herself for a healthy pregnancy. For this, it is necessary that a woman follows a healthy diet even before pregnancy. Eating healthy, balancing your nutrition such that you get the best inside you as well as having a variety of delectable and wholesome food is the key to having a problem-free pregnancy. There are therefore three important stages in a to-be-mother's life:

Diet before conception

Diet during the entire duration of pregnancy and;

Diet after delivery

During the days when there were joint families and the household was ruled by the elderly and experienced ladies, a woman got hands-on advice from them on how to look after herself and what to eat and what not to eat. But now, with more and more families becoming nuclear, a prospective mother has to depend on her physician and books to guide her.

Under the guidance of a dietary expert, we've put together a set of recipes that will take care of all the nutritional requirements during various stages of pregnancy without compromising on the taste. However do take your doctor's advice first before you embark on this special journey. Especially if there is any condition that requires a special diet, it needs to be strictly followed.

All the recipes in this book are for four portions keeping in mind that each recipe forms a part of a menu. It is also absolutely necessary to remember that one should maintain good hygiene when the food is being prepared for or consumed by an expectant mother. I would also like to add here that the popular belief that a pregnant women should be eating for two is just a myth. Overeating causes discomfort to anyone especially to a pregnant woman. So eat right, be healthy, and enjoy your pregnancy to the hilt. For, once the baby is born, life is going to be a lot busier.

Happy cooking!

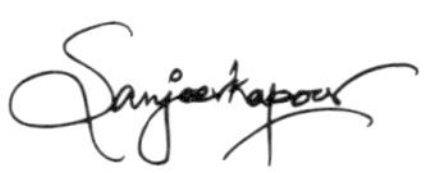

Sanjeev Kapoor

CONTENTS

Pre and Post Pregnancy Diet 7

Beverages

Amrud ka Sherbet 12
Dried Fruit Milkshake 13
Ginger Lemonade 14
Banana and Fig Milkshake 15
Carrot and Tomato Smoothie 16
Hari Chutney ki Lassi 17
Kokum Sherbet 18

Soups and Salads

Apple and Pumpkin Soup 20
Chicken and Spinach Salad 21
Cream of Broccoli Soup 22
Fresh Fruit Chaat 23
Tomato Egg-Drop Soup 24
Gajar Akhrot Kishmish ka Salad 25
Chicken and Sweet Potato Salad 26
Orange and Broken Wheat Salad 27
Chicken Shorba 28
Leafy Salad with Fruit 29
Chicken Broth 30
Mixed Sprouts Salad 31
Chicken, Coriander and Corn Soup 32
Tuna Salad 33

Snacks and Starters

Baked Handvo 35
Grilled Chicken Sandwich 36
Banana French Toast 37
Masala Omelette 38
Barbecued Mango Chicken 39
Matar Palak ka Hara Bhara Kabab 40
Barley Chicken Nuggets 41
Methi Khakhra with Bajra 42
Cheese and Sprout Sandwich 43
Mixed Vegetables, Corn and Barley Upma 44
Chicken Seekh Kabab 45
Mooli ka Muthia 46
Chicken Tikka Chaat 47
Oats Cheela with Sprouts Filling 48
Fish Fingers 49
Vegetable Idli 50
Fish Tempura 51
Vegetable Yogurt Rolls 52

Maincourse Vegetarian

Baby Corn Manchurian 54
Kale Masoor, Chawli ke Patton ke Saath 55
Baingan ka Bharta 56
Khattu Mag 57
Baked Mushroom and Nut Crumble 58
Lauki aur Wadiyon ki Sabzi 59
Bean Curd with French Beans in Hoisin Sauce 60
Masaledaar Aloo, Paneer and Broccoli 61
Bharwan Karele with Paneer 62
Methi Moong Dal 63
Bhindi Anardana 64
Paneer Bhurji 65
Chorchori 66
Potato Pepper Bake 67
Guar ane Laal Bhopla nu Shaak 68
Sai Bhaji 69
Kale Chane ki Kadhi 70
Vegetable au Gratin 71

Maincourse Non-Vegetarian

Baked Eggs and Rice 73
Fish in Foil 74

CONTENTS

Bangda Udad-Methi 75
Fish in Sweet and Sour Sauce 76
Bengali Fish Curry 77
Keema Matar 78
Char-Grilled Herbed Chicken 79
Marmalade Chicken 80
Chicken in Mushroom Lemon Sauce 81
Methiwali Machchi 82
Chicken in Tamarind and Tomato Sauce 83
Oven Baked Eggs with Creamy Vegetables 84
Chicken Stew with Easy Garlic Bread 85
Pan Seared Fish with Lemon Sauce 86
Egg Curry with Spinach 87

Rice, Noodles and Pasta

Green Mango and Peanut Rice 89
Anda Parantha 90
Hare Pyaaz aur Aloo ka Parantha 91
Barbecued Chicken Lasagne 92
Brown Rice with Chicken and Cinnamon 93
Jowar-Bajre ki Roti 94
Chicken Keema Pulao 95
Koki 96
Curd Rice 97
Mushroom Dum Biryani 98
Fada ni Khichdi 99
Pasta with Chicken and Cherry Tomatoes 100
Fettucine in Creamy Pesto Sauce 101
Spinach, Mushroom and Egg Fried Rice 102
Five-Spice Noodles and Vegetable Stir-Fry 103

Accompaniments

Aamer Chaatni 105
Beetroot Raita 106
Amla Murabba 107
Tomato Chutney 108
Angoor aur Khajur ki Chutney 109
Cucumber Raita with Flax Seeds 110
Tomato Rasam 111

Sweets and Desserts

Anjeer aur Khajur ki Burfi 113
Black Currant Ice Cream 114
Apple Rabdi 115
Brown Bread and Butter Pudding with Plum Compote 116
Badami Sheera 117
Caramel Custard 118
Baked Mango Cheesecake 119
Chocolate Chip and Oat Cookies 120
Banana and Walnut Muffins 121
Gaur Papdi 122

Annexure 123
Glossary 125
Measurements 127

PRE AND POST PREGNANCY DIET

Diet During Pregnancy

Adequate nutrition before and during pregnancy provides greater potential for a long term health impact than it does at any other time. Therefore, we must ensure that the diet which we adopt makes our journey towards getting pregnant and going through a healthy pregnancy easier.

Smart food choices are the cornerstone for pregnancy nutrition:

We need to start preparing for the pregnancy, about a year in advance. Our body needs to be nourished and swept of all the diseases and discomforts before we welcome the 'newcomer'. Though, we do need to top up the required relevant supplements (calcium and folic acid) but along with these supplements, we need to build a strong foundation by eating a well-balanced diet, rich in carbohydrates, proteins and essential fats. It is only then, that these supplements work appropriately.

Recommended dietary allowances of a pregnant woman (ICMR):

Nutrient	Normal Adult Woman	Pregnant Woman	Major Sources
Energy (kCal)	1875 – 2925 (depending on the level of activity)	+300	Cereals, millets, potato, arbi etc.
Protein (gms) (helps to maintain muscles, produces extra blood, manufactures cells, enzymes and hormones)	50	+15	Milk, yogurt, cottage cheese, buttermilk, eggs, meat, fish, dals, sprouts, roasted chana etc. Raw or undercooked meat, unpasteurised milk and raw eggs should be avoided.
Fat (gms) (they improve the women's blood pressure, blood clotting and immune response)	20	+10	Olive oil, peanut oil, mustard oil, rice bran oil and sunflower oil. Almonds, walnuts, flax seeds, groundnuts and other nuts are rich in omega 3 fatty acids, which are required for baby's vision and brain growth. Fatty fish like sardines, tuna, mackerel, herring and trout are good sources of omega 3 fatty acids. The source of fish is important, as fish from polluted waters might contain mercury which is harmful for the mother as well as the child.
Calcium (mg) (builds baby's bones and teeth)	400	+600	Milk and its products, green leafy vegetables, nachni, rajgira etc. Vitamin D from exposure to sunlight without sun tan cream. If adequate calcium is not taken by the mother, than the calcium needed by the baby is drawn from the mother's body, putting her at risk of osteoporosis.

Nutrient	Normal Adult Woman	Pregnant Woman	Major Sources
Folic Acid (mcg) (it prevents anaemia, spina bifida, premature delivery and other neural tube defects)	100	+300	Dark leafy greens, asparagus, broccoli, citrus fruits, beans (esp. soyabean), peas and lentils, lady's finger, seeds and nuts, beets, til, corn, celery, carrots, cauliflower.
Vitamin B12(mcg)	1	same	Seafood
Iron (mg) (produces haemoglobin and builds up iron reserves of the baby that lasts till 4 months of age)	30	+8	Liver, dals, dried fruits, green vegetables, eggs, enriched cereals, iron fortified salt etc. To improve the absorption of iron, eat vitamin C rich foods like amla, guava, lemon etc. at the same time. Coffee and tea with meals inhibit iron absorption in the body, hence should be avoided.
Vitamin A (mcg)	600	same	Liver, egg yolk, butter, dark green and yellow vegetables and fruits.
Thiamin (mcg)	0.9 - 1.2	+0.2	Whole grains, nuts, yeast.

General dietary recommendations:

The following are the general thumb rules to be followed by pregnant women, though the diet may need to be varied as per individual problems. One must strive to eat/drink:

- 3 cups of milk. This will build the calcium levels as we lose four times the amount of calcium that is normally lost in menstruation.
- 2 servings of meat, fish, poultry, eggs or dal.
- A dark green leafy/yellow vegetable.
- 2-3 servings of citrus fruits.
- 8 glasses of water intake to avoid urinary tract infection as well as constipation.
- Not more than 2 cups of caffeine containing beverages.
- Cheese, paneer, toast with peanut butter, a handful of bhuna chana/peanuts or flax seeds or mixed nuts, homemade white butter make for nutritious snacks.
- Essential fatty acids need to be provided through til oil, groundnut oil, coconut oil, homemade ghee, homemade unsalted butter, flax seeds, olives, egg yolk or fatty fish such as salmon and sardines. This helps in the growth and development of brain of the baby.
- Incorporate dal khichdi made out of different cereals like dalia, ragi, quinoa, jowar, rajgira etc., and vegetables in your main course, especially dinner.
- Having milk at bed time (if tolerated) aids good sleep.
- Lunch should be had by 1- 1.30 pm and dinner, preferably by 7 pm.
- Stick to homemade meals or snacks which are devoid of preservatives and other chemicals.
- Six small meals are better tolerated than three big meals.
- Cooking methods like steaming, baking, pressure cooking etc. should be employed to reduce nutrient losses and break the monotony of everyday cooking.
- Sprouting and malting are very good for improving the nutritive value and digestibility of grains.
- Good oral hygiene needs to be maintained as better teeth and chewing can prevent urinary tract infections.
- The salads and fruits should be hygienically prepared.

General dietary problems:

Nausea and vomiting: During 6th -14th weeks of pregnancy, small frequent meals with less fat are better tolerated. Main sources of energy should be whole cereals. Also excessive intake of spicy food, tea, coffee and seasonings should be restricted. Babies develop the vital body organs by the end of first trimester. Brain, lungs and other important growth of the baby depends on the kind of diet you take in your first trimester. Therefore ensure small meals which are made calorie and nutrient-dense with essential fats, sprouting and malting. Snacks like khakhra, biscuits, murmura, toast, lemon water etc. are better tolerated.

Constipation: It can be taken care of by drinking adequate quantity of water and using natural laxatives such as cereals like oats, whole wheat flour based foods and 5-6 servings of fruits and vegetables daily. Adequate sleep and exercise are also essential for proper elimination.

Oedema and leg cramps: These can be avoided by reducing the intake of milk (a high calcium and phosphate drink) and supplementing it with non-phosphate and non high calcium drinks. Magnesium also relieves leg cramps.

Heart burn: Acid reflux can be avoided by limiting the food quantity taken at one go. Drinking fluids between meals and sitting upright for at least two hours after a meal, before lying down helps.

Cravings: These are generally for sweets and dairy products. The best thing to do is include the foods that are right for you and find healthy replacements for those that may be harmful.

Some suggested foods:

- Dairy, khoya and products like milk, curd, cheese, paneer etc.
- Banana, leafy vegetables and whole grain cereals.
- Fruit based salads.
- Omelettes, boiled eggs, scrambled eggs, liver curry.
- Rice flakes (poha) and puffed rice (murmura) based snacks.
- Green gram, dal, pakoda (in the first two trimesters), bread pudding, carrot halwa.
- Pickles (if the woman does not suffer from acidity), rasam and sour foods.

Myths and realities:

Pregnancy is surrounded by myriad myths and unfounded beliefs. To top it, we Indians have a penchant for superstitions and speculations. Let us throw light on a few of them:

- **Myth - When you're pregnant, you have to eat for two.**
- Fact - During pregnancy dietary demands definitely increase. For example caloric intake needs to be increased by 300 calories, which can be met by increasing servings of cereals, dals and fruits (1-2). We need not take that extra helping of ice cream or chocolate. Eating sensibly before and throughout the pregnancy helps build up adequate reserves to provide the growing foetus with adequate nutrition.
- **Myth - Vegetables like brinjal and green leafy vegetables cause diarrhoea, hence they are better avoided.**
- Fact - The truth is that they are rich in nutrients like vitamin A, iron, folic acid, fibre and calcium which are so necessary during pregnancy. However care has to be taken to clean the vegetables properly before preparation and consumption.
- **Myth - Coconut water and some other fluids cause cold, cough and congestion.**
- Fact - This is baseless as fluids hydrate our body, prevent urinary tract infection and replenish lost minerals like potassium.
- **Myth - Dals cause bloating or arthritis, if consumed during pregnancy.**
- Fact - This is not true as dals are rich in proteins, which are the basic building blocks needed for the growing foetus.

- **Myth - Sweeping or mopping the floor in the last month helps in quick delivery.**
- Fact - The protruding uterus puts pressure on the back. Therefore, one might end up straining body parts like hip, lower back, knees etc. Therefore a sensible activity which the body can bear should be introduced.
- **Myth - Ghee is important because it will make the baby strong and will also make the delivery easy.**
- Fact - Though ghee provides us with essential fatty acids required for proper brain tissue development of the foetus, it should be had in limited amounts - one to two teaspoons per day - otherwise it will only cause unwanted increase in the weight of the mother.
- **Eating certain foods will lead to abortion.**
- Fact – Though some foods like papaya, pineapple and eggs are banned for pregnant women, fact is that as long as these fruits are ripe, they can be had safely as they fulfil the nutritional requirements that pregnancy demands. Research has indicated though, that eating raw papaya can cause uterine contractions due to the presence of enzyme papain and thus can be a little unsafe. However as far as eggs are concerned, if procured from a good source and well cooked, and you do not have an allergic history, they should be eaten as they not only fulfil the protein requirement but are rich in folic acid and vitamin A as well.

Pointers to trimester-wise nutrition:

Ist Trimester (1-3 months) - Features of this trimester are:

- Morning sickness, nausea and vomiting.
- Folic acid should be started a month prior to the conception. These aspects have been dealt in the beginning.

IInd Trimester (4-6 months) - Features of this phase:

- Gain in weight.
- Increased requirement of protein, calories, calcium, iron and other nutrients.

IIIrd trimester (7-9 months) - Features of this phase:

- Rapid increase in weight of the foetus and mother.
- Increased requirement of protein, calories, vitamins and minerals.
- Heart burn, reflux and acidity.
- Increased fluid requirements.

Besides good nutrition, working out or yoga improves your health physically, mentally and emotionally. Therefore, consult a fitness expert for appropriate workout regime that will go a long way in preparing your body for delivery as well as bring you back in shape post delivery. Furthermore, a good sleep regime is an integral part of the whole preparation and process of pregnancy. It ensures a good hormonal balance and pacifies your overworked body.

Finally, it is you who know your body better than anybody else. Therefore, listen to your own self, rather than going by what someone else 'experienced'. Discipline in terms of portion size, timings of meals and the knowledge about what you should eat, will not only help you sail through one pregnancy but also the subsequent ones, with immense ease. This is the least you can do to give your baby the best start in life.

BEVERAGES

AMRUD KA SHERBET

Guavas are high in dietary fibre, vitamin A, vitamin C, potassium, folate, copper and manganese - all of which are very beneficial for both the mother and the growing foetus.

Ingredients

2 large guavas (amrud), chopped
¼ cup sugar
2 inches ginger, grated
1 tablespoon Chaat Masala (page 123)

Method

1. Place the chopped guavas in a thick-bottomed non-stick pan along with the sugar and one and a half cups of water.
2. Bring it to a boil and simmer till the guavas are tender. Cool completely and transfer into a blender jar. Add the ginger and blend into a purée. Add the chaat masala and stir.
3. Fill half of each glass with the pulp and top up with chilled water and serve immediately.

Calories: 123.75
Carbohydrates: 29
Protein: 1.12
Fibre: 6.5
Iron: 0.337

DRIED FRUIT MILKSHAKE

Milk, dried fruit, vanilla ice cream – all things delicious and nice, what more can you ask for?

Ingredients

4 cups chilled milk

4 scoops vanilla ice cream

1 cup mixed nuts, powdered

10 tablespoons powdered sugar

Method

1. Pour the milk into a blender jar; add the vanilla ice cream, powdered nuts and sugar and blend till smooth.
2. Pour into individual glasses and serve immediately.

Calories: 655.75

Carbohydrates: 132.75

Protein: 10.85

Fat: 11.52

Fibre: 7.9

Iron: 3.9

Folic Acid: 27

GINGER LEMONADE

Ginger helps in digestion and during pregnancy some women do need a booster to help digest. During such times this drink is very beneficial.

Ingredients

2 inches ginger, grated

3 tablespoons lemon juice

1 cup sugar

4 lemon slices

Method

1. Combine the ginger and sugar with two cups of water in a deep non-stick pan. Bring the mixture to a boil, stirring continuously, until the sugar dissolves. Simmer for three minutes.
2. Strain the syrup through a piece of muslin into a bowl and set aside to cool.
3. Combine the syrup with two-and-a-half cups of chilled water and mix well. Add the lemon juice and stir till well blended.
4. Pour into individual tall glasses. Decorate each glass with a lemon slice. Serve immediately.

Calories: 250, **Carbohydrates:** 62.5

BANANA AND FIG MILKSHAKE

Loaded with Vitamin B6 which is ever so necessary for the development of the baby's central nervous system.

Ingredients

- 3 ripe bananas, peeled and chopped
- 12 dried figs, soaked, drained and chopped
- 3½ cups chilled milk
- 2 tablespoons sugar
- 2 tablespoons honey

Method

1. Place the bananas and figs in a blender jar; pour half the milk and blend till smooth.
2. Add the sugar, honey and the remaining milk and blend again.
3. Pour into individual glasses and serve immediately.

- **Calories:** 335.5
- **Carbohydrates:** 59.1
- **Protein:** 7.5
- **Iron:** 0.05

CARROT AND TOMATO SMOOTHIE

Why just pregnant women, anybody can benefit from this soothing drink. Rich in beta-carotene, this combination of carrot and tomato is excellent for well-being.

Ingredients

- 8 medium carrots, cut into 1-inch cubes
- 12 medium tomatoes, quartered
- 1 celery stalk, chopped
- Salt to taste
- 1 teaspoon black pepper powder
- 4 tablespoons lemon juice

Method

1. Place the carrots and tomatoes, in separate bowls, in the freezer till the vegetables are completely frozen.
2. Place the frozen tomatoes in a blender jar and blend for a few seconds. Add the frozen carrot cubes and blend again.
3. Add the celery, salt and pepper powder and blend till smooth.
4. Add the lemon juice and blend for a few seconds more.
5. Pour into individual stemmed glasses and serve immediately.

Calories: 157
Carbohydrates: 28.05
Protein: 4.35
Fibre: 4.65
Iron: 4.044
Folic Acid: 112.5

HARI CHUTNEY KI LASSI

Many pregnant women go through bouts of nausea and vomiting in early pregnancy. Fresh coriander and mint help to settle this to a great extent.

Ingredients

12-15 fresh mint, chopped

¼ medium bunch (50 grams) fresh coriander, chopped

2½ cups chilled yogurt

½ inch ginger, chopped

1 green chilli, chopped

½ small unripe mango, peeled, seeded and sliced

Salt to taste

Black salt to taste

1 teaspoon roasted cumin powder

Method

1. Place the chopped mint, chopped coriander, ginger, green chilli, unripe mango, salt, black salt and roasted cumin powder into a blender jar. Add one-fourth cup of water (you can use whey from the yogurt) and grind to a fine chutney.
2. Add the yogurt and one cup of water and blend again.
3. Pour into individual glasses and serve chilled.

Calories: 80.5
Carbohydrates: 4.5
Protein: 4.28
Fat: 10
Fibre: 0.15
Iron: 0.49
Folic Acid: 13.27

KOKUM SHERBET

Kokum is native to the Konkan coast, where it is extensively used to add flavour and taste to various dishes, especially fish preparations. Besides it is also rich in Vitamin C which is considered good for an expectant woman.

Ingredients

- 100 grams kokum rinds
- ¾ cup sugar
- ¼ teaspoon salt
- ½ teaspoon roasted cumin powder

Calories: 185

Carbohydrates: 46.25

Method

1. Heat three-fourth cup of water in a deep non-stick pan. Add the sugar and when the mixture comes to a boil reduce heat to medium. Cook, stirring frequently, till you get a syrup of one-string consistency.
2. Meanwhile, place the kokum in a blender jar, add one-fourth cup of water and blend to a purée.
3. Add this purée to the sugar syrup and continue to boil for two to three minutes more.
4. Take the pan off the heat, add the salt and roasted cumin powder and mix well. Set aside to cool down to room temperature.
5. To serve, pour one-fourth cup of the kokum syrup into each individual glass, top it up with chilled water and stir. Serve immediately.

Chef's Tip:

To test if the sugar syrup has reached the one-string consistency, place a drop of the syrup between your thumb and forefinger and pull them apart. If the syrup forms a single string, it is ready.

SOUPS AND SALADS

APPLE AND PUMPKIN SOUP

A recent study says that an expectant mother who eats apples, may be protecting her baby from developing wheezing and asthma.

Ingredients

- 1 golden apple, cut into cubes
- 250 grams red pumpkin, cut into cubes
- 1 cup orange juice
- Salt to taste
- 1 bay leaf
- ½ teaspoon freshly crushed black peppercorns
- ½ cup fresh cream
- A few sprigs of fresh coriander

Method

1. Cook together the apple, pumpkin, orange juice, salt and bay leaf in a deep non-stick pan on high heat. Once it comes to a boil, lower the heat, cover and cook till both apple and pumpkin are completely soft and mashed.
2. Let the mixture cool. Remove the bay leaf and blend the rest to a purée. Pass the purée through a strainer into a pan. Add two cups of water and stir and bring to a boil.
3. Adjust salt and add freshly crushed peppercorns and mix well. Lower the heat and add the fresh cream.
4. Pour into individual bowls and serve piping hot garnished with the fresh coriander sprigs.

Calories: 92.75

Carbohydrates: 10.3

Protein: 0.987

Fat: 5.15

Fibre: 0.92

Iron: 0.45

Folic Acid: 8.125

CHICKEN AND SPINACH SALAD

Besides vitamins and minerals, chicken contains lean proteins and 9 essential amino acids which are essential for the development of muscles.

Ingredients

2 boneless skinless chicken breasts

8-10 fresh baby spinach, hand torn

1 tablespoon oil

Salt to taste

¼ teaspoon crushed black peppercorns

1 sprig fresh rosemary, finely chopped

3-4 fresh basil, finely chopped

2 sprigs fresh thyme, finely chopped

4 teaspoons olive oil

2 teaspoons lemon juice

¼ teaspoon white pepper powder

¼ teaspoon sugar

5-6 green olives

5-6 black olives

5-6 stuffed olives

1 small bunch (100 grams) fresh lettuce, hand torn

Method

1. Pat the chicken breasts dry with an absorbent kitchen towel.
2. Marinate the chicken in a mixture of the oil, salt, crushed peppercorns and half of each fresh rosemary, basil and thyme. Place in the refrigerator for an hour.
3. To prepare the dressing, mix together the olive oil, lemon juice, salt, white pepper powder, sugar and the remaining fresh herbs.
4. Pre-heat a grill or non-stick tawa on medium heat. Cook the chicken breasts, turning once or twice, for five to seven minutes or till done, ensuring that the chicken breasts remain juicy.
5. Take them off the heat and set aside to cool. Cut into one-inch pieces and place them in a bowl.
6. Add the green, black and stuffed olives, lettuce, spinach and the dressing. Toss lightly and serve immediately.

Calories: 161.25
Carbohydrates: 1.4
Protein: 3.297
Fat: 11.31
Fibre: 0.27
Iron: 1.12
Folic Acid: 18.65

CREAM OF BROCCOLI SOUP

Broccoli is a good source of folic acid (folate), which is ever so necessary for the normal growth of tissue. It also contains Vitamin C, which is a powerful antioxidant and helps relieve cold symptoms. Moreover it helps the absorption of iron.

Ingredients

350 grams broccoli, separated into small florets

2 teaspoons butter

10 garlic cloves

1 medium onion, chopped

1 bay leaf

1 medium potato, finely chopped

4 cups Vegetable Stock (page 123)

Salt to taste

Black pepper powder to taste

1 cup milk

1 small red capsicum, chopped

1 teaspoon dried mixed herbs

Method

1. Heat one teaspoon of butter in a non-stick pan. Crush five garlic cloves and add to the butter. Sauté till translucent. Add the onion and bay leaf and continue to sauté for a minute.
2. Add the potato, vegetable stock, salt and pepper powder. When the mixture comes to a boil, cover and cook till the potato is done. Remove the bay leaf and add the broccoli florets. Stir and bring it to a boil again. Simmer for two minutes.
3. Using a hand blender, blend the mixture to a smooth purée. Alternatively you can take it off the heat and then blend in a blender till smooth. Add the milk and bring it to a boil.
4. Heat the remaining butter in another non-stick pan. Chop the remaining garlic cloves and add along with the red capsicum, mixed herbs and sauté for half a minute.
5. Pour the soup into individual soup bowls; garnish with the red capsicum-garlic mixture and serve piping hot.

Calories: 134.75

Carbohydrates: 23.6

Protein: 5.92

Fat: 2.69

Fibre: 3.53

Iron: 1.64

Folic Acid: 80.25

FRESH FRUIT CHAAT

An excellent snack that can be enjoyed in between the meals. So much better than any of the junk food a lot of women crave.

Ingredients

- 2 kiwi fruits, cut into 1-inch cubes
- ½ cup pomegranate kernels
- ½ cup orange segments
- ½ cup sweet lime segments
- 1 medium apple, cut into 1-inch cubes
- ¼ cup halved green grapes
- ¼ cup halved black grapes
- ½ teaspoon red chilli powder
- 1½ tablespoons Chaat Masala (page 123)
- Rock salt to taste
- 1 tablespoon lemon juice

Method

1. Place the kiwi, pomegranate kernels, orange, sweet lime, apple, green and black grapes in a large bowl and place in the refrigerator to chill thoroughly.
2. Just before serving sprinkle the chilli powder, chaat masala and rock salt. Add the lemon juice and toss well. Serve immediately.

Calories: 96.5

Carbohydrates: 36.97

Protein: 1.65

Fat: 0.15

Fibre: 4.29

Iron: 1.03

Folic Acid: 16.4

TOMATO EGG-DROP SOUP

Vitamin C which is found in abundance in tomatoes is one of the many essential nutrients needed during pregnancy to keep both the mother and the baby healthy. It not only forms healthy bones, teeth and gums, it also helps in the absorption of iron, which is so important during pregnancy.

Ingredients

- 4 medium tomatoes, chopped
- 2 eggs
- 2 teaspoons oil
- 1 medium onion, finely chopped
- 1 inch ginger, finely chopped
- 7-8 garlic cloves, chopped
- Salt to taste
- ½ teaspoon white pepper powder
- 4 tablespoons tomato ketchup
- 3½ cups Vegetable Stock (page 123)
- 2 tablespoons cornflour
- 2 tablespoons white vinegar
- 1 tablespoon sugar
- 1 tablespoon chopped fresh coriander

Method

1. Heat the oil in a deep non-stick pan. Add the onion and sauté lightly. Add the ginger and garlic and mix well. Add the tomatoes and mix.
2. Add the salt, pepper powder, tomato ketchup and mix well. Add three cups of vegetable stock and stir. Cook till the tomatoes are soft.
3. Break the eggs into a bowl and beat well. Set aside.
4. Mix the cornflour in remaining half cup of vegetable stock.
5. Add the cornflour mixture to the soup and cook till it thickens slightly. Add the vinegar and sugar and mix well.
6. Drop the beaten egg into the soup in a thin stream and mix gently till the egg coagulates and rises to the top.
7. Add the chopped coriander and mix. Serve piping hot.

Calories: 142.5

Carbohydrates: 17.3

Protein: 4.62

Fat: 5.75

Fibre: 0.885

Iron: 1.275

Folic Acid: 21

GAJAR AKHROT KISHMISH KA SALAD

Dried fruits contain higher levels of antioxidants than the fresh fruits. Besides being high in fibre they help in keeping the digestive system working smoothly, therefore they are highly recommended during pregnancy.

Ingredients

4-5 large carrots (gajar), thickly grated

½ cup chopped walnuts (akhrot)

½ cup raisins (kishmish)

2 tablespoons lemon juice

¼ teaspoon crushed black peppercorns

1 green chilli, chopped

1 tablespoon honey

Salt to taste

¼ teaspoon black salt

1 teaspoon oil

6-8 fresh mint

Method

1. Refrigerate the thickly grated carrots till required.
2. Combine the lemon juice, crushed peppercorns, green chilli, honey, salt, black salt, walnuts, raisins and oil to make a dressing.
3. Just before serving, add the dressing to the grated carrots and toss. Serve garnished with the fresh mint.

Calories: 273.75

Carbohydrates: 33

Protein: 3.65

Fat: 13.275

Fibre: 2.5

Iron: 3.58

Folic Acid: 13.5

CHICKEN AND SWEET POTATO SALAD

Both dieticians and doctors recommend the inclusion of chicken in the diet of pregnant women since it is a highly nutritious food full of vitamins and minerals and low in fat.

Ingredients

- 2 boneless chicken breasts, boiled
- 2 large sweet potatoes, boiled
- 4 tablespoons Mayonnaise (page 124)
- 1 teaspoon French mustard
- ¼ teaspoon white pepper powder
- ½ teaspoon sugar
- Salt to taste
- 150 grams cottage cheese, cut into ½-inch cubes
- 2 spring onion greens, chopped

Method

1. Cut the boiled chicken into matchstick-sized strips and set aside. Peel the boiled sweet potatoes and cut into half-inch cubes and set aside.
2. Mix together the mayonnaise, French mustard, white pepper powder, sugar and salt in a blender jar and blend at high speed until smooth. Transfer the mixture into a large bowl.
3. Add the chicken, sweet potato, cottage cheese and spring onion greens and toss well.
4. Serve chilled.

Calories: 343.25
Carbohydrates: 40.15
Protein: 20.57
Fat: 10.9
Fibre: 1.12
Iron: 0.3
Folic Acid: 3.4

ORANGE AND BROKEN WHEAT SALAD

Oranges are known to have high Vitamin C content and broken wheat has considerable amounts of fibre, minerals and vitamins – a combination of these two ingredients make a highly nutritious salad.

Ingredients

- 2 medium oranges, peeled, segments separated and seeded
- 4 tablespoons broken wheat
- 4 spring onions with greens
- 1 cup chopped fresh parsley
- 1 tablespoon chopped fresh mint
- 1 medium tomato
- 1 tablespoon lemon juice
- Salt to taste
- 1 teaspoon sugar
- ¼ teaspoon black pepper powder
- 2 teaspoons extra virgin olive oil
- 1 tablespoon toasted black sesame seeds

Method

1. Soak the broken wheat in one cup of water for about fifteen minutes. Drain and place in a deep bowl.
2. Chop the spring onion bulbs and greens separately.
3. Add the spring onion bulbs to the broken wheat and mix, crushing the onions lightly with your fingers.
4. Add the parsley and mix. Add the spring onion greens and chopped mint and mix well.
5. Quarter the tomato, scoop out the seeds and cut the flesh into small pieces. Add to the salad. Add the orange segments and toss well.
6. To make the dressing, mix together the lemon juice, salt, sugar and pepper powder. Pour over the salad and mix well. Drizzle the extra virgin olive oil and toss.
7. Chill and serve garnished with the black sesame seeds.

Calories: 207.25

Carbohydrates: 33.68

Protein: 5.42

Fat: 6.15

Fibre: 1.75

Iron: 4.04

Folic Acid: 16.63

CHICKEN SHORBA

Lot of pregnant women go through bouts of nausea when they have very little appetite for solid foods. During such times this shorba provides adequate nutrition and peps up the appetite.

Ingredients

500 grams chicken bones
100 grams boneless chicken, cut into ½-inch cubes
1 medium onion, roughly chopped
1 medium carrot, roughly chopped
1 bay leaf
4 black peppercorns
2 cloves
1 black cardamom
4 green cardamoms
1 inch cinnamon
2 tablespoons butter at room temperature
2 tablespoons refined flour
1 tablespoon oil
½ teaspoon cumin seeds
1 teaspoon crushed fennel seeds
10 garlic cloves, chopped
½ teaspoon white pepper powder
Salt to taste

Method

1. Clean and wash the chicken bones.
2. Boil four-and-a-half cups of water in a deep non-stick pan on high heat. Add the chicken bones, onion, carrot, bay leaf, peppercorns, cloves, both the cardamoms and cinnamon and bring the mixture to a boil again. Continue to boil for twenty minutes or till the water is reduced to two-and-a-half cups. Strain and set the stock aside.
3. Heat one tablespoon of butter in another non-stick pan. When the butter melts, add the chicken and sauté till they get cooked and become tender. Drain and set aside.
4. To make the roux, melt the remaining butter in the same pan. Add the flour and sauté for one to two minutes. Set aside.
5. Heat the oil in another deep non-stick pan. Add the cumin seeds, fennel seeds and garlic. Sauté for one minute, lower heat to medium, add the roux, the reduced chicken stock, white pepper powder and salt. Cook, stirring continuously, and let the mixture come to a boil on high heat.
6. Lower heat to medium, add the cooked chicken and simmer the soup for three to four minutes. Transfer into individual soup bowls and serve hot.

Chef's Tip: You may add half a cup of fresh cream just before serving to make it a little rich.

Calories: 149 **Carbohydrates:** 12.82 **Protein:** 7.175 **Fat:** 10.025 **Fibre:** 0.31 **Iron:** 0.35 **Folic Acid:** 5.4

LEAFY SALAD WITH FRUIT

Fruit and leafy vegetables are so full of essential nutrients and fibre that it is but natural that they should form a part of any healthy diet, especially so during pregnancy.

Ingredients

- ½ small (50 grams) bunch lettuce, torn into bite-sized pieces
- 2 medium apples, cut into ½-inch cubes
- 6 red grapes, seeded and quartered
- 1 medium green capsicum, cut into ½-inch pieces
- 1 medium cucumber, cut into ½-inch cubes

Dressing

- 1 tablespoon lemon juice
- ½ teaspoon red chilli flakes
- Salt to taste
- 1 teaspoon crushed black peppercorns
- 2 tablespoons extra virgin olive oil

Method

1. To make the dressing, mix together the lemon juice, chilli flakes, salt, crushed peppercorns and extra virgin olive oil.
2. Place the apples, grapes, capsicum and cucumber along with the lettuce leaves in a deep bowl. Pour the dressing over and toss.
3. Serve immediately.

Calories: 120.8
Carbohydrates: 11.05
Protein: 0.7
Fat: 7.8
Fibre: 1.05
Iron: 1.235
Folic Acid: 0.15

CHICKEN BROTH

Chicken contains unsaturated and saturated fatty acids. Best part about the chicken is that it is low in fat and therefore does not cause obesity.

Ingredients

2 boneless chicken breasts, diced

2 medium carrots, chopped

2 medium onions, chopped

1 medium potato, chopped

1 tablespoon butter

2-3 garlic cloves, chopped

¾ cup chopped fresh spinach

¾ cup milk

Salt to taste

½ teaspoon black pepper powder

Method

1. Place the chicken, carrots, onions and potato with five cups of water in a pressure cooker. Close the lid and cook till pressure is released twice (two whistles).
2. Open the lid when the pressure reduces completely. Remove the chicken and blend the remaining ingredients till smooth. Set aside.
3. Heat the butter in a deep non-stick pan and sauté the garlic for thirty seconds. Add the spinach and sauté for two minutes.
4. Add the broth, chicken and let the mixture boil for a few minutes.
5. Add the milk, salt, pepper powder and mix.
6. Pour into individual bowls and serve piping hot.

Calories: 189.1

Carbohydrates: 20.65

Protein: 15.34

Fat: 4.2

Fibre: 1.125

Iron: 1.175

Folic Acid: 20.45

MIXED SPROUTS SALAD

It is well known that sprouts are full of goodness but during pregnancy ensure that they are cooked. And yes do not go overboard, for remember moderation is the key.

Ingredients

½ cup sprouted green gram

½ cup sprouted whole Bengal gram, boiled

¼ cup sprouted chickpeas, boiled

1 medium onion, finely chopped

1 medium cucumber, cut into ½-inch cubes

1 medium green capsicum, cut into ½-inch pieces

2 medium tomatoes, seeded and cut into ½-inch pieces

1 tablespoon lemon juice

1 green chilli, slit

Salt to taste

1 teaspoon Chaat Masala (page 123)

½ cup chopped fresh coriander

Method

1. Heat one cup of water in a non-stick pan; add the sprouted green gram and cook on medium heat for two minutes. Drain and transfer into a bowl.
2. Add the sprouted boiled Bengal gram and chickpeas, mix and chill in the refrigerator for half an hour.
3. Transfer the sprouts into a large mixing bowl; add the onion, cucumber, capsicum and tomatoes and toss lightly. Add the lemon juice, green chilli, salt and chaat masala. Toss well.
4. Serve garnished with the chopped coriander.

Chef's Tip: You can also use blanched whole green gram instead of chickpeas.

Calories: 101.8
Carbohydrates: 11.87
Protein: 4.17
Fat: 0.61
Fibre: 2.66
Iron: 1.42
Folic Acid: 26.3

CHICKEN, CORIANDER AND CORN SOUP

This combination of chicken, coriander and corn brings with it all the essential nutrients that are necessary for the healthy development of a baby.

Ingredients

125 grams skinless and boneless chicken breast, cut into small cubes

3 tablespoons chopped fresh coriander

1 cup cream-style sweetcorn

4 cups Chicken Stock (page 123)

Salt to taste

White pepper powder to taste

2 tablespoons cornflour, mixed in ¼ cup water

2 egg whites, whisked lightly

Method

1. Cook the chicken in four cups of boiling chicken stock or water for five minutes.
2. Add the sweetcorn and continue to boil. Add the salt and white pepper powder and boil for two minutes.
3. Lower the heat and add the cornflour mixture and stir continuously till the mixture comes to a boil again. Add the chopped coriander and mix well.
4. Add the egg whites and stir gently.
5. Pour into individual bowls and serve piping hot.

Calories: 58.8

Carbohydrates: 9.65

Protein: 10.86

Fat: 0.831

Fibre: 1.05

Iron: 0.4

Folic Acid: 2.77

TUNA SALAD

Tuna fish is a nutrient-dense food being an excellent source of high quality protein; minerals like selenium, magnesium and potassium; the B Vitamins - niacin, B1 and B6; and also the beneficial omega-3-essential fatty acids.

Ingredients

- 1 cup drained and flaked tuna
- 3 pickled onions, chopped
- 2 inches celery stalk, chopped
- 4 tablespoons Mayonnaise (page 124)
- 3 tablespoons tomato ketchup
- 2 teaspoons red chilli sauce
- 1 small yellow capsicum, cut into 1-inch cubes
- 1 small red capsicum, cut into 1-inch cubes
- White pepper powder to taste
- 8 lettuce leaves, hand torn
- Salt to taste

Method

1. Place the tuna in a bowl. Add the pickled onions, celery, mayonnaise, tomato ketchup, red chilli sauce, yellow and red capsicums, white pepper powder and mix.
2. Chill the salad in the refrigerator for thirty minutes.
3. Arrange the torn lettuce leaves in a bowl. Add the salt to the salad and toss. Put the salad over the lettuce leaves and serve.

Chef's Tip: Pregnant women are advised to consume tuna only once a month or so as it contains mercury. Also since tinned tuna are preserved in brine, it is not recommended for hypertensive pregnant women.

Calories: 165.025, **Carbohydrates:** 18.79, **Protein:** 13.58, **Fat:** 2.7, **Fibre:** 2.01, **Iron:** 3.28

SNACKS AND STARTERS

BAKED HANDVO

Dals provide plenty of proteins which are the building blocks for baby's growth and tissue repair.

Ingredients

1 cup rice
¼ cup skinless split green gram
¼ cup split Bengal gram
¼ cup skinless split black gram
¾ cup sour yogurt
Salt to taste
2 tablespoons grated carrots
2 tablespoons grated cabbage
2 tablespoons grated bottle gourd
2 tablespoons oil + for greasing
2 teaspoons mustard seeds
2 dried red chillies, broken
2 tablespoons toasted sesame seeds
A pinch of asafoetida
8-10 curry leaves
1½ teaspoons red chilli powder
½ teaspoon turmeric powder
½ teaspoon soda bicarbonate (baking soda)

Method

1. Preheat the oven to 180°C/350°F/Gas Mark 4.
2. Dry grind the rice and the three types of gram separately. Mix together in a bowl. Add the yogurt, one and a half cups of warm water and salt and mix well. Cover and keep in a warm place to ferment overnight.
3. Add the carrots, cabbage, bottle gourd and mix well.
4. Heat two tablespoons oil in a non-stick pan and add the mustard seeds. As they begin to splutter, add the chillies, sesame seeds, asafoetida and curry leaves and sauté for a few seconds. Add the chilli powder, turmeric powder and take the pan off the heat.
5. Add the seasoning to the batter and mix well. Check for the salt. Add the soda bicarbonate and mix well.
6. Grease a six-inch square mould. Pour the batter into it till half full. Bake in the preheated oven for fifty minutes.
7. Cool slightly and remove from mould. Cut into pieces and serve with ketchup.

Calories: 440.75
Carbohydrates: 65.85
Protein: 15.1
Fat: 14.4
Fibre: 0.85
Iron: 3.08
Folic Acid: 54.6

GRILLED CHICKEN SANDWICH

Grilling gives chicken that extra flavour which will be highly appreciated by expectant mothers since they often crave for something different.

Ingredients

- 300 grams boneless chicken breasts, thinly sliced
- 8 slices brown bread
- Salt to taste
- 8-10 garlic cloves, chopped
- 1½ teaspoons red chilli flakes
- 1½ teaspoons dried mixed herbs
- 2 teaspoons olive oil
- 4 tablespoons Mayonnaise (page 124)
- 2 tablespoons tomato ketchup
- 4-5 lettuce leaves, shredded
- Butter, for grilling

Calories: 296.5
Carbohydrates: 29.175
Protein: 22.8
Fat: 9.6
Fibre: 0.1
Iron: 0.55
Folic Acid: 5.1

Method

1. Marinate the chicken in a mixture of salt, garlic, red chilli flakes and dried mixed herbs for ten to fifteen minutes.
2. Heat the olive oil in a non-stick grill pan. Place the marinated chicken on it and grill till golden brown on both the sides. Take it off the heat and set aside to cool.
3. Shred the chicken into small pieces. Add the mayonnaise, tomato ketchup and mix well. Add the shredded lettuce and mix well.
4. Preheat a sandwich griller.
5. Place the mixture on four bread slices and cover with the remaining bread slices.
6. Apply butter on top of the prepared sandwiches and grill in the preheated sandwich griller till golden brown and crisp.
7. Cut into triangles and serve.

BANANA FRENCH TOAST

Bananas are very good for expectant mothers because they are of considerable nutritional value. A single banana provides a third of the daily need of added calories. Bananas offer a variety of vitamins and minerals that are essential during pregnancy. Besides bananas are fat-free, cholesterol-free, which means they are good for the heart.

Ingredients

4 ripe bananas
4 eggs
8 bread slices
4 tablespoons butter, melted
8 tablespoons honey
½ cup fresh cream

Method

1. Peel the bananas and cut into half-inch thick slices.
2. Heat two tablespoons butter in a non-stick pan. Add the bananas and sauté for a couple of minutes. Add four tablespoons of honey to the bananas and mix.
3. Break the eggs into a bowl and beat them. Add the cream and remaining honey and mix well.
4. Heat the remaining butter in another non-stick pan.
5. Dip the bread slices in the egg mixture one by one and fry in the butter, turning sides, till golden brown on both sides. Remove onto a plate.
6. Place a French toast on a serving plate, put some banana mixture over it. Place another toast over the fruits at an angle. Put some banana mixture over the top toast and serve.

Calories: 578
Carbohydrates: 77.15
Protein: 11.9
Fat: 23.45
Fibre: 0.5
Iron: 2.16
Folic Acid: 39

MASALA OMELETTE

Besides more than 12 vitamins and minerals, eggs contain lots of quality protein, which is essential during pregnancy not only for the growing foetus but also for the mother.

Ingredients

- 8 eggs
- 2 medium onions, chopped
- 2-3 green chillies, chopped
- 1 medium tomato, chopped
- 4 tablespoons chopped fresh coriander
- Salt to taste
- 4 teaspoons oil
- Pav to serve

Method

1. Break the eggs into a large bowl. Add the onions, chillies, tomato, chopped coriander and salt and beat well with an egg beater or a fork.
2. Heat one teaspoon of oil in a non-stick pan. Pour one-fourth of the egg mixture into the pan and spread evenly.
3. Cook the eggs over medium heat for two to three minutes or till the eggs are set and the underside of the omelette is pale gold.
4. Flip over and cook again for one minute. Serve hot immediately with pav.

Calories: 247.75
Carbohydrates: 6.4
Protein: 13.8
Fat: 18.1
Fibre: 0.5
Iron: 2.55
Folic Acid: 78.5

BARBECUED MANGO CHICKEN

Unripe mango is an effective home remedy for morning sickness. Eating unripe mango with little salt can help reduce nausea during pregnancy. Unripe mango is a wonderful source of vitamin C, vitamin A and vitamin E, that enhances human hormonal system. It also relieves constipation.

Ingredients

6 tablespoons unripe mango purée

400 grams boneless chicken, cut into ½-inch cubes

4 tablespoons fresh coriander leaves paste

8-10 garlic cloves, crushed

2 teaspoons red chilli flakes + for sprinkling

¼ teaspoon clove powder

¼ teaspoon cinnamon powder

4 teaspoons brown sugar

Salt to taste

Oil for brushing

2 tablespoons butter

Method

1. Combine together the chicken, three tablespoons mango purée, coriander leaves paste, garlic, one teaspoon red chilli flakes, clove powder, cinnamon powder, one teaspoon brown sugar and salt in a bowl. Mix well and set aside for fifteen to twenty minutes to marinate.
2. Thread the marinated chicken pieces onto satay sticks.
3. Heat a non-stick grill pan and brush with oil. Place the satay sticks on it and drizzle the leftover marinade over them. Cook, rotating the sticks, till the chicken is done and evenly golden.
4. To make the sauce, heat the butter in a non-stick pan. Add each of the remaining brown sugar, mango purée and red chilli flakes. Mix well and cook till the sugar melts.
5. Sprinkle a few red chilli flakes on the barbecued chicken and serve with the mango sauce.

Calories: 208.5

Carbohydrates: 7

Protein: 25.15

Fat: 8.15

Fibre: 0.275

Folic Acid: 6.8

MATAR PALAK KA HARA BHARA KABAB

There are no two opinions that green peas are good for pregnant women for they are not only rich in proteins but also have considerable amounts of calcium and phosphorus and moreover are low in fat.

Ingredients

¾ cup shelled green peas (matar), boiled and mashed

1 cup blanched and chopped fresh spinach leaves (palak)

3 medium potatoes, boiled, peeled and grated

2 green chillies, chopped

2 tablespoons chopped fresh coriander

1 inch ginger, chopped

1 teaspoon Chaat Masala (page 123)

Salt to taste

2 tablespoons cornflour

2 tablespoons oil

Method

1. Place the peas, spinach and potatoes in a deep bowl and mix well.
2. Add the chillies, chopped coriander, ginger, chaat masala and salt and mix well. Add the cornflour and mix into a smooth and soft dough.
3. Divide the spinach mixture into twelve equal portions. Shape each portion into a ball and then press it between your palms to give it a flat round shape that looks like a thick disc.
4. Heat one teaspoon of oil in a non-stick pan. Place six kababs at a time on the pan, keeping a little distance between each. Drizzle one teaspoon oil all around the kababs and cook for two to three minutes or till the underside is golden brown. Then, turn each over and drizzle more oil all around and cook till the other side becomes golden brown. Drain on absorbent paper.
5. Serve immediately.

Calories: 185.25

Carbohydrates: 24.35

Protein: 3.92

Fat: 7.8

Fibre: 1.68

Iron: 0.93

Folic Acid: 7.8

BARLEY CHICKEN NUGGETS

Barley pearls are good for pregnant women because they prevent urinary tract infections. They also have useful proteins and vitamins B1 and B2.

Ingredients

½ cup pearl barley, soaked overnight and drained
1 cup minced chicken
2 medium onions
12 garlic cloves
½ cup roughly chopped fresh coriander
Salt to taste
Black pepper powder to taste
3 tablespoons refined flour
1 egg
½ cup cornflakes
1 cup dry breadcrumbs
Oil for shallow-frying

Method

1. Roughly chop the onions and put into a blender jar. Add the garlic, chopped coriander, minced chicken, barley, salt and pepper powder and grind till well blended. Add the refined flour and egg and blend again.
2. Transfer into a bowl, cover with a cling film and keep in the freezer for fifteen to twenty minutes.
3. Crush the cornflakes; mix with the breadcrumbs and place the mixture on a plate.
4. Remove the minced chicken from the freezer and shape into sixteen small nuggets, roll in the cornflakes-breadcrumb mixture and press lightly. Refrigerate for ten minutes.
5. Heat sufficient oil in a non-stick pan.
6. Place a few nuggets at a time and cook till the underside is golden brown. Turn over and cook till the other side is equally golden brown.
7. Serve hot with chilli sauce or tomato ketchup.

Calories: 331
Carbohydrates: 42.375
Protein: 18.675
Fat: 9.11
Fibre: 0.81
Iron: 1.3
Folic Acid: 20.27

METHI KHAKHRA WITH BAJRA

Khakhra makes a wonderful in-between meal snack. And when it is made with the nutrient dense fenugreek leaves, it is all the more desirable.

Ingredients

- 2 tablespoons fresh fenugreek leaves (methi), chopped
- 2 tablespoons millet (bajra) flour
- ½ cup wholewheat flour
- ¼ teaspoon ginger-garlic paste
- ¼ teaspoon turmeric powder
- ½ teaspoon red chilli powder
- 2 tablespoons oil
- Salt to taste
- Ghee, for roasting

Method

1. Combine the millet flour, wholewheat flour, ginger-garlic paste, turmeric powder, chilli powder, oil, salt and fenugreek leaves in a deep bowl. Add half a cup of water and knead into a soft dough.
2. Divide the dough into eight equal portions and roll out each portion into a five-inch diameter thin chapati.
3. Heat an iron tawa. Cook each chapati on both the sides with a little ghee until light golden.
4. With the help of a thick wad made with folded kitchen towels, press the chapati on all the sides and roast on low heat till it is crisp. This is khakhra.
5. Cool and store in an air-tight container.

Calories: 239.5, **Carbohydrates:** 16.375, **Protein:** 2.8, **Fat:** 18.06, **Fibre:** 0.35, **Iron:** 1.39, **Folic Acid:** 8.9

CHEESE AND SPROUT SANDWICH

Sprouts are rich in proteins but raw sprouts should be avoided by pregnant women since they may also have harmful bacteria. So long as they are blanched they are an excellent food for an expectant mother.

Ingredients

- 24 tablespoons grated processed cheese
- 1 cup sprouted green gram, blanched and drained
- 8 slices brown bread
- 1 medium onion, chopped
- 2 medium potatoes, boiled, peeled and mashed
- Salt to taste
- Green Chutney (page 123), as required
- 1 teaspoon Chaat Masala (page 123)
- 12-16 black peppercorns, crushed
- 8-10 lettuce leaves
- 2 medium tomatoes, cut into round slices
- 4 teaspoons butter
- Tomato ketchup, for serving

Method

1. Place the onion, mashed potatoes, salt, two tablespoons green chutney, chaat masala, crushed peppercorns and sprouts in a bowl and mix well. Divide into four equal portions.
2. Heat a sandwich griller.
3. For each sandwich, place one brown bread slice on the work top. Place one or two lettuce leaves and spread one portion of the sprouts mixture on the bread slice. Place the tomato slices and sprinkle one tablespoon grated cheese on top of the sprouts mixture.
4. Apply a little green chutney on another slice and place it over the cheese layer with the chutney side facing down.
5. Place the sandwiches, two at a time, in the sandwich griller and toast till crisp. Apply a little butter on top and serve with tomato ketchup.

Calories: 303.525

Carbohydrates: 48.93

Protein: 10.49

Fat: 7.3

Fibre: 1.37

Iron: 2.05

Folic Acid: 30.1

MIXED VEGETABLES, CORN AND BARLEY UPMA

Corn is very rich in folic acid which is very essential for a pregnant woman since its deficiency can cause the infant to be underweight and may also lead to neural tube defects at birth. Yellow corn is rich in beta-carotene that provides the body with vitamin A, which is essential for the maintenance of good vision and healthy skin.

Ingredients

- 1 small carrot, cut into small cubes
- 5-6 French beans, chopped
- ¼ cup shelled green peas, blanched
- ½ cup sweet corn kernels, boiled and lightly crushed
- ½ cup pearl barley
- 1 tablespoon ghee
- ¼ teaspoon cumin seeds
- 1 medium onion, chopped
- 1 green chilli, slit
- ½ inch ginger, grated
- Salt to taste
- 2 tablespoons chopped fresh coriander

Method

1. Soak the barley in two cups of water for half an hour. Drain and set aside.
2. Heat the ghee in a pressure cooker. Add the cumin seeds. When they begin to change colour, add the onion, chilli and ginger and sauté till the onion becomes soft.
3. Add the carrot, French beans, barley and salt. Sauté for two to three minutes.
4. Add one and half cups of water. Cover the cooker with the lid and cook till the pressure is released once (one whistle). Open the lid when the pressure has reduced completely. Add the green peas and corn kernels and mix. Place on heat and cook for one minute.
5. Garnish with the chopped coriander and serve hot.

Calories: 645, **Carbohydrates:** 103.6, **Protein:** 18.9, **Fat:** 16.9, **Fibre:** 22, **Iron:** 4.7, **Folic Acid:** 84

CHICKEN SEEKH KABAB

Chicken is rich in protein, iron and other nutrients which are necessary during the pregnancy.

Ingredients

500 grams minced chicken

1-2 green chillies, finely chopped

1 medium onion, finely chopped

1 inch ginger, finely chopped

4 garlic cloves, finely chopped

2 tablespoons finely chopped cashew nuts

1 teaspoon Chaat Masala (page 123)

1 teaspoon Garam Masala powder (page 123)

1 teaspoon white pepper powder

2 tablespoons chopped fresh coriander

1 tablespoon lemon juice

Salt to taste

Oil, as required

2 tablespoons butter

Method

1. Mix together the minced chicken, green chillies, onion, ginger, garlic, cashew nuts, chaat masala, garam masala powder, white pepper powder, chopped coriander, lemon juice and salt in a bowl.
2. Alternatively, you can use boneless chicken and grind it together with the green chillies, onion, ginger and garlic. Add the remaining ingredients except the oil and butter and mix.
3. Heat a non-stick tawa and drizzle some oil on it. Wet your palms; take a little chicken mixture and pat it around a satay stick. Press firmly and place the seekh kababs on the tawa. Cook, turning from time to time, so that they cook evenly all around. Baste with butter at regular intervals.
4. Serve hot.

Calories: 185.75, **Carbohydrates:** 2.5, **Protein:** 13.22, **Fat:** 13.45, **Fibre:** 0.135, **Iron:** 0.15, **Folic Acid:** 4.9

MOOLI KA MUTHIA

Radishes have essential nutrients, fibre and water. Only make sure they are washed thoroughly before consuming them as they may carry certain bacteria that are harmful.

Ingredients

- 1 cup grated radish (mooli)
- ½ cup chopped radish greens
- ½ cup coarse wholewheat flour
- ½ cup gram flour
- ¾ cup sorghum flour
- 2 tablespoons yogurt
- 4 tablespoons chopped fresh coriander
- 1 teaspoon lemon juice
- 6 teaspoons oil
- 2 teaspoons green chilli-ginger paste
- ½ teaspoon turmeric powder
- 1 tablespoon sugar
- Salt to taste
- 2 pinches soda bicarbonate (baking soda)
- 1 teaspoon mustard seeds
- 8-10 curry leaves
- ¼ teaspoon asafoetida
- 1 teaspoon sesame seeds

Method

1. Combine together the radish, radish greens, flour, gram flour, sorghum flour, yogurt, two tablespoons chopped coriander, lemon juice, two teaspoons oil, green chilli-ginger paste, turmeric powder, sugar, salt and soda bicarbonate in a bowl and knead into a soft dough.
2. Apply a little oil on your palms and divide the mixture into four portions.
3. Shape each portion into six-inch long and one-inch thick cylinders.
4. Arrange the rolls (muthia) on a greased flat stainless steel colander and steam in a steamer for twenty to twenty-five minutes. Take the steamer off the heat and set aside.
5. Cool the muthia slightly and cut into half-inch thick slices.
6. Heat two teaspoons oil in a non-stick kadai and add the mustard seeds and curry leaves. When the seeds begin to splutter, add the asafoetida and sesame seeds.
7. Add the muthia pieces and sauté on medium heat for two to three minutes or till they are light brown and crisp.
8. Serve hot garnished with the remaining chopped coriander.

Calories: 260.62, **Carbohydrates:** 40.45, **Protein:** 8.14, **Fat:** 7.35, **Fibre:** 1.2, **Iron:** 2.82, **Folic Acid:** 13.51

CHICKEN TIKKA CHAAT

Pregnant women often crave for something sour and this has adequate amounts of yogurt and unripe mango to satiate that craving.

Ingredients

2 boneless chicken breasts (approx. 300 grams), skinned and cubed
1 teaspoon Kashmiri red chilli powder
1 teaspoon ginger paste
1 teaspoon garlic paste
1 cup drained (hung) skimmed milk yogurt
Salt to taste
½ teaspoon Garam Masala Powder (page 123)
2 tablespoons lemon juice
3 teaspoons olive oil
1 small green capsicum, diced
1 small red capsicum, diced
1 small yellow capsicum, diced
1 medium onion, sliced
2 green chillies, chopped
1 teaspoon Chaat Masala (page 123)
2 tablespoons chopped fresh coriander
½ small unripe mango, chopped (optional)

Method

1. Combine together the chilli powder, ginger and garlic pastes, yogurt, salt, garam masala powder, one tablespoon lemon juice and two teaspoons of olive oil in a bowl.
2. Add the chicken and mix well. Set aside to marinate for three to four hours, preferably in the refrigerator.
3. Preheat an oven to 200°C/400°F/Gas Mark 6. Alternatively, preheat a tandoor.
4. Thread the chicken pieces onto skewers and cook in the preheated oven (or a moderately hot tandoor), for ten to twelve minutes, or until almost done. Baste the chicken with the remaining oil and cook for another four minutes. Set aside to cool. Remove the chicken from the skewers.
5. Combine the chicken tikka with the capsicums, onion, chillies, chaat masala, half the chopped coriander, the remaining lemon juice and the mango (if using), and toss well.
6. Transfer into a serving dish and serve garnished with the remaining chopped coriander.

Calories: 310.75

Carbohydrates: 21.7

Protein: 28.92

Fat: 10.27

Fibre: 3.135

Iron: 0.77

Folic Acid: 19.1

OATS CHEELA WITH SPROUTS FILLING

Oats provide dietary fibre, protein and iron which are necessary nutrients to be included in the diet of a pregnant woman.

Ingredients

Cheela batter

½ cup rolled oats
1¼ cups gram flour
2 green chillies, chopped
½ teaspoon red chilli powder
¼ teaspoon turmeric powder
½ teaspoon carom seeds
3 tablespoons yogurt
1 tablespoon chopped fresh coriander
Salt to taste
Oil for shallow-frying
Butter, as required

Filling

1 cup green gram sprouts, blanched and drained
1 tablespoon oil
2 medium onions, chopped
2 medium tomatoes, seeded and chopped
¼ teaspoon turmeric powder
½ teaspoon red chilli powder
½ teaspoon Chaat Masala (page 123)
Salt to taste
1 teaspoon lemon juice
1 tablespoon chopped fresh coriander

Method

1. To make the cheela batter, mix together the oats, gram flour, chillies, chilli powder, turmeric powder, carom seeds, yogurt, chopped coriander and salt. Add one and one-fourth cups of water and whisk to a smooth batter of pouring consistency. Let it rest for ten to fifteen minutes.
2. To make the filling, heat the oil in a non-stick pan; add the onions and sauté for two minutes. Add the tomatoes and cook till pulpy.
3. Add the sprouts and continue to sauté for half a minute. Add the turmeric powder, chilli powder, chaat masala, salt, lemon juice and chopped coriander and sauté for one minute. Take the pan off the heat and set aside.
4. Heat a non-stick tawa; grease it with a little oil and pour a little batter on it. Spread into a thin round with the back of a ladle. Drizzle a little oil all around and cook till the underside becomes golden brown. Turn over, drizzle a little oil all around and cook till the other side is equally golden brown.
5. Place a portion of the stuffing on one side, fold the other side over to make a half-moon shape. Serve hot with a dollop of butter.

Calories: 330.75, **Carbohydrates:** 34.5, **Protein:** 9.93, **Fat:** 24.375, **Fibre:** 2.45, **Iron:** 2.89, **Folic Acid:** 23.05

FISH FINGERS

Fish is very nutritious as it is rich in protein and omega-3-fatty acids, besides it has few calories.

Ingredients

- 400 grams rawas fish fillets
- 1 tablespoon ginger paste
- 1 tablespoon garlic paste
- Salt to taste
- 2 tablespoons lemon juice
- ½ cup coarse rice flour
- 2 teaspoons red chilli powder
- Oil for deep-frying

Method

1. Cut the fish fillets into three-inch by half-inch by half-inch fingers.
2. Marinate the fish fingers in a mixture of ginger paste, garlic paste, salt and lemon juice for half an hour.
3. Mix together the coarse rice flour, chilli powder and salt and place in a plate.
4. Remove the fish fingers from the marinade and roll them in the rice flour mixture.
5. Heat sufficient oil in a non-stick kadai and deep-fry till crisp and done. Drain on absorbent paper.
6. Serve hot with garlic chutney.

Calories: 359
Carbohydrates: 15.025
Protein: 12.525
Fat: 25.625
Fibre: 0.025
Iron: 0.9

VEGETABLE IDLI

An ideal breakfast item for pregnant women as we all know that vegetables are good sources of vitamins and minerals and should be an important part of their daily diet.

Ingredients

- 1 cup parboiled rice
- ½ cup skinless split black gram
- Salt to taste
- 1 medium carrot, grated
- 4-5 French beans, chopped
- 2-3 cauliflower florets, grated
- ½ medium green capsicum, chopped
- 2 tablespoons oil
- 1 inch ginger, finely chopped
- 15-20 black peppercorns, crushed
- 2 tablespoons chopped fresh coriander

Method

1. Soak the rice and split black gram separately for at least four hours. Drain and grind the rice with a little water to a coarse batter; grind the split black gram with a little water to a thin batter.
2. Mix both the batters together, adding water if necessary, to make a batter of dropping consistency.
3. Add the salt; cover and leave in a warm place to ferment, overnight or for four or five hours.
4. Add the vegetables to the fermented batter and mix well.
5. Lightly grease the idli moulds with oil. Pour a spoonful of batter into each mould. Sprinkle ginger, crushed peppercorns and chopped coriander. Fit the moulds onto the idli stand.
6. Heat some water in a pressure cooker and place the idli stand in it. Cover the cooker with the lid and steam, without the weight, for ten minutes, or till done.
7. Serve hot with chutney.

Calories: 273.9

Carbohydrates: 56.395

Protein: 10.09

Fat: 0.6

Fibre: 0.93

Iron: 1.35

Folic Acid: 38.07

FISH TEMPURA

Mothers who eat fish during pregnancy have children with better physical and cognitive development.

Ingredients

- 400 grams rawas fish fillets, cut into 1-inch pieces
- ½ teaspoon white pepper powder
- Salt to taste
- Juice of ½ lemon
- 1 teaspoon Thai red curry paste
- ¾ cup refined flour
- ½ cup cornflour
- ¼ teaspoon baking powder
- ¾ cup oil + for deep-frying

Method

1. Place the fish in a bowl; add the white pepper powder, salt, lemon juice and red curry paste and toss well. Chill in the refrigerator for about fifteen minutes.
2. Mix together the refined flour, cornflour, baking powder, three-fourth cup oil, salt and three-fourth cup of chilled water. Whisk thoroughly to make a batter of pouring consistency. Set aside for twenty minutes.
3. Heat sufficient oil in a wok. Dip the fish pieces, one by one, in the batter and deep-fry on medium heat, turning frequently or until crisp and golden brown. Drain on absorbent paper.
4. Serve hot.

Calories: 673
Carbohydrates: 28.05
Protein: 18.8
Fat: 451.25
Iron: 2.025
Folic Acid: 2.5

VEGETABLE YOGURT ROLLS

These wonderfully tasty rolls are healthy too, what with a medley of vegetables and yogurt adding their nutrients.

Ingredients

½ medium zucchini, sliced

1 medium carrot, sliced

1 medium green capsicum, cut into thick strips

2 medium onions, quartered and layers separated

8-10 fresh spinach leaves, shredded

½ cup yogurt

4 roti

2 tablespoons tahini

2 tablespoons Green Chutney (page 123)

Salt to taste

5-6 fresh mint, hand torn

3 tablespoons olive oil

2 teaspoons lemon juice

1 teaspoon mixed herbs

1 teaspoon red chilli flakes

A few sprigs of fresh parsley, chopped

Method

1. Mix the tahini, yogurt, green chutney, salt and fresh mint in a small bowl and set aside.
2. Marinate the zucchini, carrot, green capsicum and onions in olive oil, lemon juice, mixed herbs, chilli flakes and salt for about fifteen minutes.
3. Grill the vegetables on a hot grill till the grill marks are seen on the pieces. Take off from heat and set aside. Divide into four portions.
4. Place one roti on the work table; apply the tahini mixture, sprinkle the shredded spinach, arrange one portion of vegetables, sprinkle the parsley and roll it up. Make the other rolls similarly.
5. Serve immediately.

Calories: 341.05

Carbohydrates: 63.645

Protein: 11.83

Fat: 5.16

Fibre: 2.9

Iron: 4.56

Folic Acid: 57.1

MAINCOURSE VEGETARIAN

BABY CORN MANCHURIAN

A pregnant woman should eat something from all the food groups in order to get proper amounts of energy. And corn is a carbohydrate that can be relished by them often.

Ingredients

- 12 baby corns, cut into 1-inch pieces
- 4 tablespoons refined flour
- 4 tablespoons cornflour
- Salt to taste
- 1 tablespoon ginger paste
- 1 tablespoon garlic paste
- 2 tablespoons oil + for deep-frying
- 5-6 garlic cloves, finely chopped
- 1 inch ginger, finely chopped
- 1 green chilli, finely chopped
- 2 spring onion bulbs, finely chopped
- 2 tablespoons soy sauce
- 2 tablespoons tomato sauce
- 2 teaspoons vinegar
- 2 stalks spring onion greens, chopped

Method

1. Mix together the baby corns, refined flour, two tablespoons cornflour and salt in a bowl.
2. Add the ginger paste and garlic paste and mix. Sprinkle some water and mix well.
3. Heat sufficient oil in a wok and deep-fry the baby corns till golden. Drain on absorbent paper and set aside.
4. Heat two tablespoons oil in another non-stick wok and add the garlic, ginger, green chilli and sauté for a few seconds. Add the spring onions bulbs and sauté for one minute.
5. Mix the remaining cornflour in four tablespoons of water. Set aside.
6. Add the soy sauce and tomato sauce to the wok and mix. Add one cup of water and bring to a boil. Add the cornflour mixture and cook till the mixture thickens.
7. Add the fried baby corns and mix well. Add the vinegar and mix.
8. Garnish with the spring onion greens and serve hot.

Calories: 294.5

Carbohydrates: 15.9

Protein: 1.45

Fat: 25.25

Fibre: 0.3

Iron: 0.35

KALE MASOOR, CHAWLI KE PATTON KE SAATH

Whole lentil is rich in protein and fibre and is also heart friendly. Just the grain to be had by pregnant women.

Ingredients

¼ cup whole lentils (kale sabut masoor), soaked

2 small bunches (250 grams each) fresh green amaranth (chawli), chopped

¼ teaspoon turmeric powder

Salt to taste

3 teaspoons oil

1 teaspoon cumin seeds

½ cup coconut milk

½ teaspoon lemon juice

Paste

1 tablespoon coriander seeds

½ tablespoon cumin seeds

6-8 garlic cloves

½ inch ginger

3 dried Kashmiri red chillies, broken

Method

1. To make the paste, place the coriander seeds, cumin seeds, garlic, ginger and dried chillies in a blender jar and grind to a smooth paste with a little water if required.
2. Pressure-cook the lentils with the turmeric powder, salt and half cup of water till the pressure is released thrice (three whistles). Set aside to cool.
3. Heat the oil in a non-stick pan and add the cumin seeds. When the seeds begin to change colour, add the green amaranth and cook for ten minutes, stirring continuously.
4. Remove the lid of the pressure cooker and transfer the lentils into the pan and mix well. Add the ground paste and cook for five to seven minutes, stirring continuously.
5. Add the coconut milk and salt and simmer for two to three minutes.
6. Take the pan off the heat, add the lemon juice and mix well. Serve hot.

Calories: 149

Carbohydrates: 13.375

Protein: 5.375

Fat: 11.7

Fibre: 1.6

Iron: 10.35

Folic Acid: 4.5

BAINGAN KA BHARTA

Brinjals have considerable amounts of Vitamin A, iron and dietary fibre – all of which are essential nutrients needed during pregnancy. However this vegetable should be consumed in moderation, especially if the mother-to-be suffers from acidity problems.

Ingredients

- 1 large (approx. 650 grams) brinjal (baingan)
- 3 tablespoons oil
- 5 large onions, chopped
- 3 medium tomatoes, chopped
- Salt to taste
- 1 teaspoon red chilli powder
- 2 tablespoons chopped fresh coriander

Method

1. Roast the brinjal directly on direct flame till it gets cooked well and the skin gets charred completely. Cool, peel and mash.
2. Heat the oil in a non-stick pan and sauté the onions till light golden brown. Add the tomatoes, salt and chilli powder, and sauté till the masala is cooked and the oil separates from the masala.
3. Add the mashed brinjal and mix well. Reduce the heat and cook for four to five minutes. Add the chopped coriander and mix well. Serve hot.

Note: It is easier to remove the charred skin of a roasted brinjal if it is dipped in water just after roasting. While buying, select a brinjal that is light in weight in proportion to its size. Add one-fourth cup of grated cauliflower or boiled green peas while sautéing the onions for variation.

Calories: 221.75
Carbohydrates: 18.45
Protein: 4.475
Fat: 12.2
Fibre: 3.4
Iron: 1.915
Folic Acid: 63.5

KHATTU MAG

Pregnant women should eat plenty of whole grains, which are rich in proteins.

Ingredients

½ cup whole green gram (mag/moong), soaked for 1 hour, drained

Salt to taste

1½ cups sour yogurt, whisked

2 tablespoons gram flour

¼ teaspoon turmeric powder

1 teaspoon ginger paste

1 teaspoon green chilli paste

1 teaspoon sugar

1 tablespoon oil

A pinch of asafoetida

½ teaspoon mustard seeds

½ teaspoon cumin seeds

3-4 cloves

1 inch cinnamon

¼ teaspoon fenugreek seeds

8-10 curry leaves

Method

1. Heat two cups of water in a deep non-stick pan. Add the green gram and salt and bring to a boil. Reduce the heat, cover and cook for fifteen to twenty minutes or till the green gram is soft.
2. Pour the yogurt into a large bowl; add the salt, gram flour, turmeric powder, ginger paste and green chilli paste and whisk well. Add the sugar and one cup of water and whisk again.
3. Heat the oil in a non-stick pan; add the asafoetida, mustard seeds, cumin seeds, cloves, cinnamon, fenugreek seeds, curry leaves and sauté till seeds begin to splutter. Add the yogurt mixture and cook for five minutes or till the gram flour gets cooked and the mixture thickens.
4. Add the green gram and cook on medium heat for three to four minutes more.
5. Take the pan off the heat and transfer into a serving bowl. Serve immediately.

Calories: 171.475

Carbohydrates: 17.7

Protein: 8.875

Fat: 10.2

Fibre: 1.025

Iron: 1.43

Folic Acid: 11.64

BAKED MUSHROOM AND NUT CRUMBLE

Mushrooms are excellent source of several vitamins, minerals and dietary fibre, low in sodium and cholesterol, it is absolutely safe to be consumed by a mother-to-be.

Ingredients

600 grams fresh button mushrooms, sliced
2 cups Vegetable Stock (page 123)
4 tablespoons butter
1 large onion, finely chopped
7-8 garlic cloves, crushed
½ cup refined flour
Salt to taste
½ teaspoon crushed black peppercorns
4 tablespoons fresh cream
2 tablespoons chopped fresh parsley

Crumble Topping

¼ cup ground almonds
¼ cup finely chopped walnuts
10-15 pistachios, finely chopped
¾ cup rolled oats
¾ cup wholewheat flour
1 teaspoon dried thyme
Salt to taste
Black pepper powder to taste
4 tablespoons softened butter
1 tablespoon fennel seeds

Method

1. Preheat an oven to 180°C/350°F/Gas Mark 4.
2. Cook the mushrooms with vegetable stock in a large non-stick pan for a few minutes or till mushrooms are just tender. Drain and reserve the stock.
3. Melt the butter in another non-stick pan and gently sauté the onion and garlic for two to three minutes or till just softened but not browned. Stir in the flour and cook for a minute.
4. Take the pan off the heat and gradually stir in the reserved mushroom stock. Return to the heat and cook stirring, until thickened. Add the mushrooms, salt, crushed peppercorns, cream and parsley and mix well. Spoon the mixture into a shallow ovenproof dish.
5. To make the topping, mix together the oats, flour, thyme, almonds, walnuts, pistachios, salt and pepper powder. Using a fork mix in the butter until the topping resembles coarse breadcrumbs.
6. Sprinkle the topping over the mushrooms, sprinkle the fennel seeds over the topping and bake in the preheated oven for twenty-five to thirty minutes or until golden and crisp.
7. Serve hot.

Calories: 561.25 **Carbohydrates:** 28.51
Protein: 15.57 Fat: 47.07 Fibre: 6.165
Iron: 27.6 Folic Acid: 21.175

LAUKI AUR WADIYON KI SABZI

The dal makes this dish rich in proteins, a nutrient that is so essential for healthy growth of a baby.

Ingredients

1 (400 grams) bottle gourd (lauki), cut into 1-inch pieces

2 black gram nuggets (urad dal wadiyaan), broken

¼ cup split Bengal gram, soaked

2 medium tomatoes, chopped

½ teaspoon turmeric powder

½ teaspoon red chilli powder

3 green chillies, broken

Salt to taste

3 tablespoons ghee

3 dried red chillies, broken

¼ teaspoon asafoetida

4-5 garlic cloves, finely chopped

1 inch ginger, chopped

1 teaspoon cumin seeds

1 teaspoon sugar

1 tablespoon chopped fresh coriander

Method

1. Drain and transfer the Bengal gram into a pressure cooker. Add the tomatoes, turmeric powder, chilli powder, green chillies, three to four cups of water and salt. Add the bottle gourd pieces. Cook till pressure is released three times (three whistles).
2. Heat the ghee in a non-stick kadai. Add the red chillies and sauté till light brown. Add the asafoetida, garlic, ginger and sauté. When the garlic turns a light brown, add the cumin seeds and sauté. Add the broken nuggets and sauté for three to four minutes.
3. Open the lid of the pressure cooker when the pressure reduces completely and whisk the dal. Pour it into the kadai and mix.
4. Add the sugar and little water to get the desired consistency and cook till it comes to a boil. Serve hot garnished with the chopped coriander.

Calories: 246.5

Carbohydrates: 23.8

Protein: 8.7

Fat: 12.15

Fibre: 1.97

Iron: 2.07

Folic Acid: 70.64

BEAN CURD WITH FRENCH BEANS IN HOISIN SAUCE

Bean curd or tofu is low in calories and high in protein and just the right ingredient to replace non-vegetarian food in vegetarian diet.

Ingredients

- 200 grams firm bean curd
- 250 grams French beans, halved
- 3 tablespoons Hoisin sauce
- 1 tablespoon rice bran oil
- 1 inch ginger, sliced
- 10 garlic cloves, chopped
- 1 medium onion, sliced
- 1 tablespoon red chilli sauce
- 1 tablespoon soy sauce
- Salt to taste

Method

1. Cut the bean curd into half-inch thick fingers.
2. Heat the oil in a non-stick wok; add the ginger and garlic and sauté for two minutes. Add the onion and sauté for two minutes more.
3. Add the Hoisin sauce and red chilli sauce and mix. Add the French beans and mix again.
4. Add the bean curd, soy sauce and salt and toss gently till heated through.
5. Serve hot.

Calories: 99
Carbohydrates: 5.41
Protein: 5.42
Fat: 6.125
Fibre: 1.26
Iron: 3.175
Folic Acid: 37.37

MASALEDAAR ALOO, PANEER AND BROCCOLI

A healthful combination of potatoes, cottage cheese and broccoli for they have almost all the nutrients that are essential for the development of a baby.

Ingredients

2 medium potatoes (aloo), parboiled, peeled and cut into cubes

200 grams cottage cheese (paneer), cut into triangles

150 grams broccoli, separated into small florets

2 tablespoons oil

1 teaspoon ginger-garlic paste

10-12 spring onion bulbs, halved, layers separated

Salt to taste

6-8 cherry tomatoes

½ teaspoon red chilli flakes

½ teaspoon black pepper powder

½ teaspoon dried oregano

Method

1. Heat the oil in a non-stick pan. Add the ginger-garlic paste and spring onions and sauté for a few minutes.
2. Add the potatoes and salt and sauté for four to five minutes more.
3. Add the broccoli and cook till the potatoes are done.
4. Add the cottage cheese, cherry tomatoes, chilli flakes, pepper powder and dried oregano and mix well. Cook for three to four minutes. Add three tablespoons of water and mix and cook for a few seconds.
5. Serve hot.

Calories: 372

Carbohydrates: 19.05

Protein: 17.15

Fat: 25.225

Fibre: 0.75

Iron: 1

Folic Acid: 24

BHARWAN KARELE WITH PANEER

Make sure to remove the seeds of the bitter gourds completely or use tender ones in which the seeds have not formed because the seeds contain a chemical which is not safe during pregnancy.

Ingredients

8 medium bitter gourds (karele)
Salt to taste
1 tablespoon oil
2 medium onions, chopped
1 teaspoon ginger paste
1 teaspoon garlic paste
2 medium tomatoes, chopped
1 teaspoon coriander powder
½ teaspoon red chilli powder
1 teaspoon cumin powder
½ teaspoon turmeric powder
2 teaspoons Tamarind Pulp (page 123)

Stuffing

250 grams cottage cheese (paneer), grated
1 teaspoon oil
1 teaspoon carom seeds
1 small onion, chopped
Salt to taste
½ teaspoon red chilli powder
¼ teaspoon Garam Masala powder (page 123)
2 tablespoons chopped fresh coriander

Method

1. Scrape and make a slit on one side of the bitter gourds and remove the seeds. Rub the salt over and inside the bitter gourds and set aside for an hour. Wash under running water and drain well.
2. To prepare the stuffing, heat the oil in a non-stick pan. Add the carom seeds and onion and sauté for a minute. Add the grated cottage cheese, salt, chilli powder, garam masala powder and mix well. Add the chopped coriander and mix.
3. Stuff this masala mixture into each bitter gourd and set aside.
4. To cook the stuffed bitter gourds, heat the oil in a non-stick kadai. Add the onions and sauté till light golden brown. Add the ginger paste and garlic paste and sauté for two minutes. Add the tomatoes and cook for two minutes. Add the coriander powder, chilli powder, cumin powder, turmeric powder and mix well and sauté till well blended.
5. Add the stuffed bitter gourds and half a cup of water and salt. Cover and cook on high heat for one to two minutes. Reduce the heat and cook for ten to twelve minutes, stirring gently at regular intervals.
6. Add the tamarind pulp and mix well. Cover again and cook for ten to fifteen minutes more or till the bitter gourds are tender.
7. Serve hot.

Calories: 288.25 **Carbohydrates:** 15.7
Protein: 15.01 **Fat:** 18.28 **Fibre:** 1.79
Iron: 1.65 **Folic Acid:** 3

METHI MOONG DAL

We already know the benefits of fresh fenugreek leaves. Here it is cooked along with split green gram which provide folate, an important nutritive ingredient needed during preconception. It also prevents neural tube defects during pregnancy.

Ingredients

280 grams fresh fenugreek (methi), chopped

¼ cup skinless split green gram (dhuli moong dal), soaked and drained

1 tablespoon oil

½ teaspoon cumin seeds

1 medium onion, chopped

3-4 garlic cloves, chopped

2 green chillies, chopped

½ teaspoon turmeric powder

Salt to taste

2 tablespoons gram flour, mixed with 2 tablespoons of water

1 teaspoon pure ghee

1 teaspoon lemon juice

Method

1. Heat the oil in a non-stick pan and add the cumin seeds. When they begin to change colour, add the onion, garlic and green chillies and sauté for a minute.
2. Add the turmeric powder, chopped fenugreek and salt and cook for five minutes.
3. Add the split green gram, gram flour mixture and mix well. Add half cup of water and bring to a boil.
4. Cover and cook for ten to fifteen minutes on low heat or till the green gram is cooked. Drizzle the pure ghee and add lemon juice. Mix well.
5. Serve hot with rice or roti.

Calories: 131.475

Carbohydrates: 15.65

Protein: 6.9

Fat: 4.025

Fibre: 1.005

Iron: 2.13

Folic Acid: 10.187

BHINDI ANARDANA

Lady's fingers are a rich source of folate, a nutrient that is very beneficial for a pregnant woman. Besides the dried pomegranate seeds add a delicious piquant taste to this dish which is savoured by most during pregnancy.

Ingredients

- 400 grams lady's fingers (bhindi), trimmed and slit
- 2 tablespoons dried pomegranate seeds (anardana)
- 3 tablespoons oil
- 1 teaspoon cumin seeds
- 4-5 green chillies, slit
- 12-15 shallots, peeled
- ¼ teaspoon red chilli powder
- ¼ teaspoon turmeric powder
- 1 teaspoon coriander powder
- 1 teaspoon dried mango powder
- Salt to taste
- ½ teaspoon Garam Masala Powder (page 123)
- ½ tablespoon lemon juice
- 1 tablespoon chopped fresh coriander

Method

1. Dry-roast the dried pomegranate seeds in a non-stick pan lightly on low heat. Spread it on the tabletop and crush with a rolling pin.
2. Heat the oil in a non-stick kadai. Add the cumin seeds. When they begin to change colour, add the green chillies and shallots and sauté till the shallots become soft.
3. Add the lady's fingers and sauté for three to four minutes. Add the chilli powder, turmeric powder, coriander powder, dried mango powder and salt and toss well.
4. When the lady's fingers are almost done add the crushed pomegranate seeds, garam masala powder and lemon juice and mix well. Add the chopped coriander and mix well.
5. Serve hot.

Calories: 145.75, **Carbohydrates:** 8.27, **Protein:** 2.1, **Fat:** 11.25, **Fibre:** 1.31, **Iron:** 0.6, **Folic Acid:** 105

PANEER BHURJI

Cottage cheese is rich in calcium but it is better made at home rather than bought ready-made.

Ingredients

- 400 grams cottage cheese (paneer)
- 3 tablespoons oil
- 2 teaspoons cumin seeds
- 3-4 green chillies, slit
- 4 medium onions, chopped
- ½ teaspoon turmeric powder
- ½ teaspoon red chilli powder
- Salt to taste
- 2 tablespoons chopped fresh coriander

Method

1. Heat the oil in a non-stick pan and add the cumin seeds and green chillies. As the cumin seeds begin to change colour, add the onions and sauté till light brown.
2. Add the turmeric powder, chilli powder and salt and stir well.
3. Crumble the cottage cheese and add and mix well. Allow to cook for two to three minutes, stirring lightly.
4. Serve hot garnished with the chopped coriander.

Calories: 416.25
Carbohydrates: 12.3
Protein: 19.5
Fat: 32.05
Fibre: 0.6
Iron: 0.6
Folic Acid: 6

CHORCHORI

All of us have days when there are small amounts of veggies of different kinds in our refrigerator. Here is a recipe that uses assorted vegetables and conjures up something tasty and bursting with nutrition. Because fruits and vegetables are created by nature such that it is easier for the expectant woman's body to break these down and use the essential nutrients optimally.

Ingredients

¼ medium cauliflower, separated into small florets

2 medium potatoes, cut into ½-inch pieces

1 medium sweet potato, cut into ½-inch pieces

100 grams red pumpkin, cut into ½-inch pieces

1 medium brinjal, cut into ½-inch pieces

6-8 French beans, cut into ½-inch pieces

6-8 fresh spinach leaves, shredded

1½ tablespoons mustard oil

1½ teaspoons Paanch Phoron (page 124)

½ teaspoon red chilli powder

¼ teaspoon turmeric powder

2 green chillies, slit

½ teaspoon sugar

Salt to taste

Method

1. Heat one tablespoon of mustard oil in a non-stick pan till it reaches smoking point. Take the pan off the heat, allow it to cool and reheat the oil on medium heat.
2. Add the paanch phoron and when the seeds start spluttering, add the chilli powder and mix.
3. Add the cauliflower, potatoes, sweet potato, pumpkin, brinjal, French beans and spinach and mix well. Add the turmeric powder, green chillies, sugar and salt. Reduce the heat, cover the pan and cook for eight to ten minutes, stirring occasionally, or till the potatoes are cooked.
4. Add the remaining raw mustard oil and cook for one minute or till all the moisture evaporates.
5. Serve hot.

Calories: 167.75

Carbohydrates: 24.37

Protein: 3.68

Fat: 6.01

Fibre: 2.1

Iron: 1.76

Folic Acid: 48.57

POTATO PEPPER BAKE

The addition of broccoli makes this dish nutrient rich as it is known for being a good source of calcium, and is also packed with vitamin C, folate, and vitamin B6.

Ingredients

8 medium potatoes

½ teaspoon black pepper powder

3 tablespoons oil

1 medium red capsicum, chopped

8-10 medium broccoli florets, finely chopped

1 medium carrot, grated

1 medium onion, chopped

5-6 garlic cloves, chopped

3 tablespoons grated cottage cheese

½ teaspoon mixed dried herbs

Salt to taste

4 tablespoons grated cheese

Method

1. Wash and dry the potatoes and prick deeply with a fork.
2. Place the potatoes on a paper towel and cook in the microwave oven, uncovered, on Microwave HIGH for five minutes. Turn the potatoes over and continue cooking for five to six minutes or till soft.
3. Remove the potatoes, halve them lengthways and scoop out the pulp leaving a thin wall all around on the inside of the skin. Mash the scooped out pulp lightly with a fork.
4. Brush a little oil over the potato skins. Arrange them in a shallow microwave-safe dish and pour a little oil around the insides also. Cook, uncovered, on Microwave HIGH for eight minutes or until the skins are crisp.
5. Place the red capsicum, broccoli florets, carrot, onion, garlic, cottage cheese and dried herbs in a small microwave-safe bowl and season with salt, pepper powder and the remaining oil. Cover and cook in the microwave oven on Microwave HIGH for five minutes until soft.
6. Mix the mashed potatoes with the vegetable mixture. Stuff the mixture into the potato skins. Sprinkle the grated cheese evenly on top.
7. Place the potato halves in a wide-mouthed microwave-safe dish, and cook in the microwave oven, uncovered, on Microwave HIGH for three minutes. Alternatively grill on TOP mode for three to five minutes. Serve immediately.

Calories: 468.3 **Carbohydrates:** 74.637
Protein: 9.175 **Fat:** 15.16 **Fibre:** 1.97
Iron: 3.765 **Folic Acid:** 70.35

GUAR ANE LAAL BHOPLA NU SHAAK

Vegetables are rich in vitamins and minerals, especially the high content of vitamin A makes them very beneficial for pregnant women.

Ingredients

- ¾ cup one-inch pieces of cluster beans (guar)
- ¾ cup cubed red pumpkin (laal bhopla)
- 1 tablespoon oil
- 1 teaspoon cumin seeds
- ½ teaspoon carom seeds
- A pinch of asafoetida
- 1 teaspoon red chilli powder
- ½ teaspoon turmeric powder
- Salt to taste
- 2 teaspoons coriander powder
- 1 teaspoon cumin powder
- 1 tablespoon chopped fresh coriander

Method

1. Heat the oil in a non-stick pan and add the cumin seeds. When they begin to change colour, add the carom seeds and asafoetida and mix.
2. Add the cluster beans, pumpkin, chilli powder, turmeric powder and salt and sauté for two to three minutes.
3. Add the coriander powder, cumin powder and mix. Add one-fourth cup of water, cover and cook for about fifteen to twenty minutes on low heat or till both the cluster beans and pumpkin are cooked.
4. Mash the pumpkin with the back of the ladle. Garnish with the chopped coriander and serve hot.

Calories: 54.25, **Carbohydrates:** 7.7, **Protein:** 2.3, **Fat:** 4,
Fibre: 0.6, **Iron:** 0.76, **Folic Acid:** 78.5

SAI BHAJI

Green leafy vegetables are chock-full of nutrients that are essential for the baby growing in the womb, and that too in tasty, easy-to-assimilate form. So just go for this popular Sindhi dish!

Ingredients

400 grams fresh spinach

½ medium bunch sorrel leaves

2 tablespoons oil

½ teaspoon cumin seeds

2 medium onions, finely chopped

1 inch ginger, finely chopped

3-4 green chillies, finely chopped

2 small long brinjals, cut into 1-inch cubes

1 small potato, peeled and cut into 1-inch cubes

4 tablespoons split Bengal gram, soaked

2 large tomatoes, roughly chopped

¼ teaspoon turmeric powder

1 teaspoon red chilli powder

Salt to taste

Method

1. Finely shred the spinach and half the sorrel leaves.
2. Heat the oil in a pressure cooker and add the cumin seeds. When they begin to change colour, add the onions and sauté till golden brown.
3. Add the ginger and green chillies, and sauté for a few seconds. Add a little water, if required.
4. Add the spinach, whole sorrel leaves, shredded sorrel leaves, brinjal and potato cubes, drained Bengal gram, tomatoes, turmeric powder, chilli powder and salt. Stir in two cups of water.
5. Cover the cooker with the lid and cook till the pressure is released once (one whistle). Reduce the heat and cook for eight to ten minutes more. Open the lid when the pressure is released completely.
6. Remove the potato cubes with a slotted spoon and blend the remaining mixture with a hand blender. Add the potato cubes and serve hot.

Calories: 213.75

Carbohydrates: 24.887

Protein: 6.9

Fat: 9.3

Fibre: 2.1

Iron: 2.7

Folic Acid: 54.7

KALE CHANE KI KADHI

With a little bit of planning, a vegetarian diet can provide all the nutrients you need for a healthy pregnancy. While planning the menu, be sure to include ingredients that are high in folate and black Bengal gram is one of them.

Ingredients

- 1½ cups black Bengal gram (kale chane), soaked overnight in 4 cups of water
- 1½ cups yogurt
- 4 teaspoons gram flour
- ¼ teaspoon turmeric powder
- Salt to taste
- 1 teaspoon red chilli powder
- 2 teaspoons coriander powder
- 1 teaspoon Garam Masala Powder (page 123)
- 3-4 green chillies, chopped
- 4 tablespoons pure ghee
- 1 teaspoon cumin seeds
- A pinch of asafoetida
- 2 tablespoons chopped fresh coriander

Method

1. Drain the Bengal gram, and pressure-cook with four cups of water till pressure is released five times (five whistles) or till done. Drain and reserve the cooking liquid. Place the Bengal gram in a bowl and mash them lightly.
2. Mix the yogurt, gram flour, turmeric powder, salt, chilli powder, coriander powder and garam masala powder in a separate bowl and whisk well till no lumps remain and the mixture attains a smooth consistency. Add the green chillies and mix. Add one cup of the reserved liquid and mix.
3. Heat the ghee in a non-stick pan and add the cumin seeds. When they begin to change colour, add the asafoetida and yogurt mixture and stir. Add the Bengal gram, adjust seasoning and add some more of the reserved liquid. Bring it to a boil and cook for five minutes.
4. Garnish with the chopped coriander and serve hot.

Calories: 450
Carbohydrates: 47.92
Protein: 15.075
Fat: 25
Fibre: 2.92
Iron: 3.64
Folic Acid: 147.47

VEGETABLE AU GRATIN

Each vegetable in this dish lends its nutrient to make it an extremely healthy one.

Ingredients

- 12-15 French beans, finely chopped
- 2 medium carrots, finely chopped
- 2 large potatoes, cut into batons
- 2 large green capsicums, sliced
- 8-10 fresh button mushrooms, chopped
- 3 teaspoons butter
- 1 large onion, thickly sliced
- 3 large tomatoes, sliced
- Salt to taste
- Black pepper powder to taste
- 2 cups White Sauce (page 124)
- ½ cup grated processed cheese

Method

1. Preheat the oven to 180°C/350°F/Gas Mark 4.
2. Heat the butter in a non-stick pan, add the onion and sauté on medium heat till soft. Add the tomatoes and sauté for one minute. Add the French beans, carrots, potatoes, capsicums and mushrooms and sauté for three to four minutes.
3. Add the salt, pepper powder and white sauce and stir to mix well.
4. Transfer the mixture into an oven-proof dish and sprinkle the cheese on top.
5. Bake in the preheated oven for ten to fifteen minutes or till the cheese turns golden brown.
6. Serve hot with bread.

Calories: 345.25, **Carbohydrates:** 39.39, **Protein:** 10.67, **Fat:** 15.8, **Fibre:** 2.7
Iron: 2.22, **Folic Acid:** 43.325

MAINCOURSE NON-VEGETARIAN

BAKED EGGS AND RICE

Egg, being a storehouse of several essential nutrients like protein, fats, minerals (like zinc and selenium) and vitamins A, D and B, is one of the most nutritious food for pregnant women. Only make sure that the eggs are fresh.

Ingredients

- 4 eggs
- 2 cups cooked rice
- 2 tablespoons butter
- 1 tablespoon olive oil
- 4-5 garlic cloves, chopped
- 1 medium onion, chopped
- 8-10 fresh button mushrooms, sliced
- 1 bunch (250 grams) fresh spinach, roughly chopped
- Salt to taste
- Black pepper powder to taste
- ½ cup fresh cream
- ¼ cup grated Parmesan cheese

Method

1. Preheat an oven to 180˚C/350˚F/Gas Mark 4.
2. Heat the butter and olive oil together in a non-stick pan. Add the garlic and onion and sauté for two minutes.
3. Add the mushrooms and allow them to soften. Add the spinach, salt and pepper powder and stir. Add the rice and mix well.
4. Add the cream and mix. Transfer the mixture into a shallow baking dish. Sprinkle half the Parmesan cheese. Make four equidistant wells in the bed of rice.
5. Break one egg into each well. Sprinkle the remaining cheese.
6. Bake in the preheated oven for five minutes or till the eggs are set. Serve hot.

Chef's Tip: Vegetarians can use soaked soya granules instead of eggs.

Calories: 459.75
Carbohydrates: 44.25
Protein: 14.77
Fat: 20.01
Fibre: 4.76
Iron: 2.15
Folic Acid: 56.69

FISH IN FOIL

With minimal spices this fish preparation is just right for an expectant mother.

Ingredients

400 grams boneless fish fillets, cut into 2-inch pieces

½ cup roughly chopped fresh coriander

10 garlic cloves

1 teaspoon red chilli flakes

Salt to taste

1 tablespoon lemon juice

4 six-inch square aluminium foil pieces

Method

1. Grind together the chopped coriander, garlic, red chilli flakes, salt, lemon juice with two tablespoons of water into a fine paste. Transfer into a bowl.
2. Add the fish and mix gently. Set aside to marinate for ten to fifteen minutes.
3. Place aluminium foil squares on the table top, put equal portion of marinated fish on each of them, fold in the edges and seal to form envelopes.
4. Heat a non-stick tawa, place the envelopes on it and cook on medium heat for two to three minutes. Turn over and cook for two to three more minutes.
5. Serve hot in the envelope itself.

Calories: 96.25

Carbohydrates: 1.025

Protein: 15.27

Fat: 0.75

Fibre: 0.1

Iron: 1.12

Folic Acid:

BANGDA UDAD-METHI

Bangda or mackerel has high levels of omega-3-fatty acids which are very good for pregnant women. They can certainly enjoy this dish once in a while.

Ingredients

4 (approx. 425 grams) mackerels (bangda), scaled and cleaned
2 tablespoons skinless split black gram (dhuli urad dal)
½ teaspoon fenugreek seeds (methi dana)
Salt to taste
3 tablespoons oil
2 tablespoons rice
5 black peppercorns
4 large onions, sliced
1 cup grated fresh coconut
4 teaspoons Tamarind Pulp (page 123)
8 dried red chillies
2 teaspoons turmeric powder

Calories: 774.5
Carbohydrates: 124.93
Protein: 24.86
Fat: 23.096
Fibre: 1.61
Iron: 6.26
Folic Acid: 21.6

Method

1. Cut each mackerel into four pieces and put them into a bowl. Rub one teaspoon salt on the fish pieces and marinate for fifteen minutes in a refrigerator. Wash under running water and place in a colander to drain off excess water.
2. Heat one teaspoon oil in a non-stick frying pan. Add the rice and sauté till it becomes dark brown. Drain and set aside to cool.
3. To the oil remaining in the pan, add the split black gram and sauté till light brown. Drain and set aside to cool. Add the fenugreek seeds and black peppercorns to the oil remaining in the pan and sauté till fragrant. Drain and set aside.
4. Transfer the sautéed rice and black gram into a mixer jar and grind to a coarse powder and set aside. Grind the sautéed fenugreek seeds and black peppercorns with one tablespoon water to a fine paste and set aside.
5. Heat two teaspoons oil in the same pan. Add one-fourth of the sliced onions and sauté till golden brown. Add the coconut and sauté till brown. Cool the mixture and grind with tamarind pulp, chillies and turmeric powder to a coarse paste and set aside.
6. Heat the remaining oil in a deep non-stick pan. Add the remaining sliced onions and sauté till the onions soften.
7. Add the coconut paste, five cups of lukewarm water and salt and stir. Add the fenugreek seed-peppercorns paste, stir and bring the mixture to a boil.
8. Add the mackerels, ground rice-black gram powder. Stir and lower the heat. Cook for three minutes or till the fish is done.
9. Serve hot with steamed rice.

FISH IN SWEET AND SOUR SAUCE

Fish is considered very high in nutrients that are necessary for a pregnant woman. Choose a fish which is low in mercury and you have nothing to worry.

Ingredients

- 400 grams boneless fish fillets, cut into 2-inch pieces
- 3 tablespoons oil
- 1 large onion, sliced
- 2 teaspoons ginger paste
- 2 teaspoons garlic paste
- 1 teaspoon cumin powder
- 2 tablespoons chopped fresh coriander
- 3 green chillies, slit
- 1 medium tomato, chopped
- Salt to taste

Sweet and Sour Sauce

- 1 tablespoon vinegar
- 1 tablespoon Worcestershire sauce
- 1 teaspoon sugar
- 1 tablespoon refined flour

Method

1. Heat the oil in a non-stick pan. Add the onion and sauté on medium heat till light brown.
2. Add the ginger paste, garlic paste, cumin powder, chopped coriander and green chillies and sauté till the mixture turns a light brown.
3. Place the fish gently in the pan and cook for a minute, gently spooning the masala over the slices. Add the tomato.
4. For the sweet and sour sauce, blend together the vinegar, Worcestershire sauce, sugar and refined flour and stir into the fish-tomato mixture.
5. Add one cup of hot water and salt to taste. Cover the pan and cook gently on very low heat for ten minutes or until the fish is cooked, with the gravy coating the slices thickly.
6. Take the pan off the heat and serve hot.

Calories: 219, Carbohydrates: 5.75, Protein: 15.725, Fat: 12.075, Fibre: 0.365, Iron: 1.34, Folic Acid: 9.15

BENGALI FISH CURRY

Resplendent with the flavour of ground mustard this fish curry is an absolute delight. The coconut milk balances the pungency of ground mustard seeds.

Ingredients

- 1 (800 grams) rohu fish, cut into ½-inch thick slices
- 1 tablespoon mustard seeds
- Salt to taste
- 2 teaspoons turmeric powder
- 1 tablespoon oil + for shallow-frying
- 6 garlic cloves
- 3 green chillies
- 1½ teaspoons onion seeds
- ½ cup coconut milk
- 2 tablespoons chopped fresh coriander

Method

1. Soak the mustard seeds in a little water for half an hour.
2. Wash the fish well and apply little salt and one teaspoon turmeric powder and set aside for fifteen minutes.
3. Heat sufficient oil in a non-stick frying pan and shallow-fry the fish pieces, turning sides, till half done. Drain and set aside.
4. Grind together the mustard seeds, garlic cloves and two roughly chopped green chillies to a smooth paste.
5. Heat one tablespoon of oil in a non-stick pan. Add the onion seeds, one slit green chilli and remaining turmeric powder. Add the ground paste and sauté for one to two minutes.
6. Add half cup of water, salt and cook till thick. Add another half cup of water and bring to a boil.
7. Add the fried fish and coconut milk and simmer for one minute. Serve hot garnished with the chopped coriander.

Calories: 392.5

Carbohydrates: 6.6

Protein: 21.87

Fat: 31

Fibre: 0.65

Iron: 1.65

KEEMA MATAR

Make sure the minced mutton is properly cooked before serving it to a pregnant woman.

Ingredients

2 cups minced mutton

½ cup shelled green peas, blanched

2 tablespoons oil

2 medium onions, chopped

1 teaspoon garlic paste

1 teaspoon ginger paste

2 green chillies, minced

1 teaspoon coriander powder

1 teaspoon cumin powder

¾ teaspoon red chilli powder

3 medium tomatoes, puréed

3 tablespoons chopped fresh coriander

Salt to taste

1 teaspoon Garam Masala Powder (page 123)

1½ tablespoons lemon juice

Method

1. Heat the oil in a deep non-stick pan; add the onions and sauté till they turn a light brown. Add the garlic paste and ginger paste and sauté for a minute.
2. Add the minced mutton, green chillies, coriander powder, cumin powder and chilli powder and sauté for five minutes, breaking up any mince lumps if formed. Add the puréed tomatoes and continue to sauté for three minutes more.
3. Add three-fourth cup of water and bring the mixture to a boil. Cover the pan with a lid, lower the heat and simmer for half an hour.
4. Remove the lid; add the green peas, chopped coriander, salt, garam masala powder and lemon juice and stir the mixture for two minutes. Add half cup of water and mix well. Cover the pan again and simmer for about ten minutes or until the peas are fully cooked.
5. Serve hot.

Calories: 272.5

Carbohydrates: 9.675

Protein: 12.47

Fat: 20.3

Fibre: 1.275

Iron: 0.99

Folic Acid: 5.87

CHAR-GRILLED HERBED CHICKEN

All the herbs make this grilled chicken extremely flavourful. But remember to go easy on the herbs for in excess they may be tasty but not beneficial.

Ingredients

- 2 boneless chicken breasts
- 2 teaspoons mixed dried herbs
- ½ tablespoon olive oil
- 2-3 garlic cloves, chopped
- 1 tablespoon chopped fresh parsley
- 1 tablespoon butter
- Salt to taste
- Crushed black peppercorns to taste
- ½ lemon

Method

1. Heat a non-stick grill pan on high heat.
2. Mix the mixed herbs with olive oil and rub the mixture all over the chicken.
3. Place the chicken on the hot grill pan and cook, turning sides, for eight to ten minutes or till done.
4. Mix the garlic, parsley, butter, salt and crushed peppercorns and drizzle over the chicken.
5. Lower the heat and squeeze the juice of half a lemon over the chicken. Cook for thirty seconds.
6. Serve hot.

Calories: 127.25
Carbohydrates: 3.375
Protein: 13.97
Fat: 6.2
Fibre: 0.8
Iron: 4.47
Folic Acid: 3.4

MARMALADE CHICKEN

Foods high in folate, such as oranges, are very good for pregnant women especially because it supports conception and the development of a healthy placenta. It is also good for the baby because it helps prevent brain or spinal cord defects.

Ingredients

- 4 chicken legs
- 4 tablespoons marmalade
- 2 inches ginger, finely chopped
- 3 garlic cloves, finely chopped
- 2 teaspoons Dijon mustard paste
- ½ teaspoon sea salt
- Black pepper powder to taste
- ¼ cup orange juice
- 1 tablespoon olive oil + for greasing
- 2 spring onion bulbs, finely chopped

Method

1. Preheat the oven to 180°C/350°F/Gas Mark 4.
2. Mix the marmalade, ginger, garlic, mustard paste, sea salt, pepper powder, orange juice and one tablespoon olive oil in a bowl. Add the chicken legs and mix again.
3. Grease a baking tray with a little oil and place the chicken legs in it. Drizzle the remaining marinade over them. Cover with an aluminium foil and bake in the preheated oven for thirty minutes or till done.
4. Serve hot garnished with the spring onions.

Calories: 358.87

Carbohydrates: 13.47

Protein: 30.25

Fat: 19.85

Folic Acid: 8.5

CHICKEN IN MUSHROOM LEMON SAUCE

B vitamins, iron, some other essential minerals, and antioxidants are packed into the seemingly small and modest mushroom, making it good for a pregnant woman.

Ingredients

- 2 boneless and skinless chicken breasts, halved
- 12-14 fresh button mushrooms, sliced
- 3½ tablespoons lemon juice
- ¼ teaspoon grated lemon zest
- 1 egg, lightly beaten
- ⅓ cup refined flour
- Salt to taste
- ½ teaspoon black pepper powder
- ¼ teaspoon red chilli flakes
- 2 tablespoons olive oil
- 1 tablespoon butter
- 2-3 garlic cloves, finely chopped
- 1 small onion, finely chopped
- ½ cup Chicken Stock (page 123)
- ¼ cup fresh cream

Method

1. Mix the egg with one tablespoon lemon juice in a bowl and set aside until required.
2. Place the flour in a bowl; add the salt, pepper powder, red chilli flakes and lemon zest and mix well.
3. Heat the olive oil in a non-stick pan over medium heat.
4. Dip the chicken breasts in the egg mixture, then roll in the seasoned flour until well coated and place on the pan.
5. Cook for five minutes on each side or until done. Drain the chicken from the pan and keep covered with aluminum foil so that they remain warm.
6. Heat the butter in the same pan; add the garlic, onion and mushrooms. Sauté for three to four minutes.
7. Mix the chicken stock, remaining lemon juice and cream in a small bowl and add to the pan. Cook till the sauce thickens.
8. Place the chicken on a serving plate; pour the sauce over the chicken and serve with boiled noodles or steamed rice.

Calories: 306.75

Carbohydrates: 19.86

Protein: 16.2

Fat: 17.31

Fibre: 0.65

Iron: 0.8

Folic Acid: 12.93

METHIWALI MACHCHI

Greens are oh-so-good for both the mother-to-be and the baby that is growing within her. Fresh fenugreek leaves are considered very good for blood formation in pregnant mothers. It not only prevents anaemia but is cooling too!

Ingredients

- 1 bunch (250 grams) fresh fenugreek (methi), chopped
- 4 black pomfret fillets (machchi)
- 1 tablespoon lemon juice
- Salt to taste
- 2 teaspoons oil
- ½ teaspoon mustard seeds
- 1 inch ginger, chopped
- 3-4 garlic cloves, chopped
- 4 spring onion bulbs, chopped
- 1 medium tomato, chopped
- 2 green chillies, chopped
- 1 medium unripe mango, peeled and chopped
- ¼ teaspoon turmeric powder

Method

1. Cut the fish fillets into one-inch pieces and put into a bowl. Add the lemon juice and salt and mix well. Marinate in the refrigerator for fifteen minutes.
2. Heat the oil in a non-stick pan. Add the mustard seeds and as they begin to splutter, add the ginger, garlic and spring onions and sauté for two minutes.
3. Add the chopped fenugreek and sauté for two to three minutes. Add the tomato, green chillies, mango and turmeric powder and cook for two minutes, stirring continuously.
4. Add half cup of water and continue to cook on high heat, stirring at regular intervals.
5. Once the gravy comes to a boil, add the marinated fish and salt to taste. Cover with a lid and cook on low heat for seven to eight minutes or till fish is tender.
6. Stir gently, adjust seasoning and serve hot.

Calories: 154.75

Carbohydrates: 27.2

Protein: 15.45

Fat: 3.6

Fibre: 0.825

Iron: 3.08

CHICKEN IN TAMARIND AND TOMATO SAUCE

Absolutely 'chatakdar', just what an expectant mother craves for.

Ingredients

750 grams chicken on the bone, cut into 1-inch pieces

2 tablespoons Tamarind Pulp (page 123)

3 medium tomatoes, chopped

1 tablespoon Garam Masala Powder (page 123)

1 teaspoon turmeric powder

Salt to taste

Black pepper powder to taste

1 medium onion, chopped

2 tablespoons sugar

4 green chillies, finely chopped

10-12 fresh mint, chopped

1 tablespoon chopped fresh coriander

2 tablespoons oil

2-3 curry leaves

2 tablespoons lemon juice

Method

1. Mix together the garam masala powder, turmeric powder, salt and pepper powder in a bowl; add the chicken and rub in the masala well.
2. Boil three cups of water in a deep non-stick pan. Add the tamarind pulp, tomatoes, onion, sugar and green chillies and cook till pulpy.
3. Add the chopped mint and chopped coriander and mix well.
4. Heat the oil in another non-stick pan. Add the curry leaves and chicken and cook for eight to ten minutes.
5. Transfer the cooked chicken into the tamarind and tomato sauce. Continue to cook on low heat for two minutes. Take the pan off the heat, add the lemon juice and mix well. Let it stand for five minutes.
6. Serve hot with chapati.

Calories: 368

Carbohydrates: 12.55

Protein: 25.89

Fat: 24.1

Fibre: 0.71

Iron: 0.62

Folic Acid: 19.25

OVEN BAKED EGGS WITH CREAMY VEGETABLES

Have this creamy and wholesomely delightful dish of vegetables and eggs with garlic bread and you will feel satiated.

Ingredients

4 eggs
4 tablespoons fresh cream
5-6 fresh button mushrooms, thinly sliced
1 medium carrot, diced and blanched
1 medium potato, diced and blanched
½ cup shelled green peas, blanched
½ cup corn kernels
3 tablespoons butter
1 medium onion, chopped
Salt to taste
¼ cup milk
¼ cup grated cheese
½ cup breadcrumbs
2 tablespoons chopped fresh parsley
1½ teaspoons red chilli flakes

Method

1. Preheat the oven to 200°C/400°F/Gas Mark 6.
2. Heat two tablespoons butter in a non-stick pan; add the onion and sauté for a minute. Add the mushrooms and sauté till light brown. Add the carrot, potato, peas and corn kernels and mix.
3. Add the salt, fresh cream, milk and cheese, mix and cook for five minutes or till well blended.
4. Mix together the breadcrumbs, parsley, red chilli flakes in a bowl, add the remaining butter and mix well.
5. Transfer the vegetables into a baking dish. Sprinkle three-fourth of the breadcrumb mixture over them. Make four small wells at equidistance.
6. Break one egg into each well. Cover with a sprinkling of the remaining breadcrumb mixture. Bake in the preheated oven for eight to ten minutes.
7. Serve hot.

Calories: 330.025

Carbohydrates: 27.1

Protein: 12.36

Fat: 19.4

Fibre: 1.685

Iron: 2.74

Folic Acid: 54.1

CHICKEN STEW WITH EASY GARLIC BREAD

Nutrient rich and easy to make it is sure to make you feel on top of the world.

Ingredients

750 grams chicken, cut into 1½-inch cubes on the bone

3 tablespoons unsalted butter

8-10 garlic cloves, sliced

2 medium onions, sliced

2 medium carrots, cut into large pieces

2 medium potatoes, cut into large pieces

3 tablespoons whole-wheat flour

Salt to taste

5 cups Chicken Stock (page 123)

½ teaspoon black pepper powder

6-8 French beans, cut into 1-inch pieces

½ cup milk

Garlic Bread

1 French loaf

4 tablespoons salted butter

2 teaspoons garlic paste

5-6 black peppercorns, crushed

Method

1. Preheat an oven to 200°C/400°F/Gas Mark 6.
2. For the garlic bread, cream the butter till smooth; add the garlic paste and crushed peppercorns. Slit the French loaf diagonally every two inches and generously apply the butter in the slits, wrap in aluminum foil and place in the preheated oven and bake for five to eight minutes.
3. To make the chicken stew, heat the butter in a non-stick pan. Add the garlic, onions, carrots, potatoes and sauté for four to five minutes on high heat or till all the moisture dries up.
4. Add the whole wheat flour and sauté for a minute. Add the chicken, salt and sauté for eight to ten minutes. Add the stock and bring to a boil. Add half the pepper powder. Cover and cook for three to four minutes.
5. Uncover, add the French beans, mix and cook. Add the milk and the remaining pepper powder. Cover and cook on medium heat for seven to eight minutes.
6. Serve hot with the hot garlic bread.

Calories: 551.5

Carbohydrates: 46.875

Protein: 31.82

Fat: 25.27

Fibre: 2.15

Iron: 2.9

Folic Acid: 81.52

PAN SEARED FISH WITH LEMON SAUCE

Fish being rich in omega-3-fatty acids are considered good for pregnant women. However, please remember that moderation is the key especially since fish have certain amounts of mercury too.

Ingredients

- 400 grams boneless fish fillets (rawas), cut into 1½-inch pieces
- 1 tablespoon lemon juice
- Salt to taste
- 1 tablespoon chopped fresh dill
- 2 tablespoons refined flour
- 2 tablespoons oil + for shallow-frying

Sauce

- 2 spring onion bulbs, sliced
- ½ cup fresh cream
- 1 tablespoon butter
- 1 tablespoon lemon juice

Method

1. Place the fish pieces in a bowl; add the lemon juice, salt, fresh dill, refined flour and oil, mix well and marinate in the refrigerator for thirty minutes.
2. Heat the oil in a non-stick pan and shallow-fry the fish till golden brown. Drain on absorbent paper and set aside.
3. To make the sauce, heat a non-stick pan; add the spring onions and cook till soft. Add the cream and bring to a boil. Take the pan off the heat and add butter. Whisk well till smooth. Add the lemon juice and mix well.
4. Arrange the sautéed fish on a serving plate and pour the sauce over it and serve immediately.

Calories: 251.5, **Carbohydrates:** 3.65, **Protein:** 15.7, **Fat:** 16.025, **Iron:** 1.05

EGG CURRY WITH SPINACH

Eggs and spinach make a great combination both from the presentation and nutrition points of view.

Ingredients

- 4 eggs, hard-boiled and peeled
- 2 medium bunches (250 grams each) fresh spinach, blanched and puréed
- 2 tablespoons oil
- 2 teaspoons ginger paste
- 4 teaspoons garlic paste
- 4 medium onions, ground
- 3 medium tomatoes, puréed
- ½ teaspoon Kashmiri red chilli powder
- ¼ teaspoon turmeric powder
- ½ teaspoon cumin powder
- 1 teaspoon coriander powder
- Salt to taste
- ¼ cup fresh cream

Method

1. Heat the oil in a non-stick pan; add the ginger paste and garlic paste and sauté for half a minute. Add the ground onions and sauté till golden brown.
2. Add the tomato purée and sauté till the oil separates. Add the spinach purée and cook for five to ten minutes, or till the raw flavour disappears.
3. Add the chilli powder, turmeric powder, cumin powder, coriander powder and salt. Mix well and sauté for two to three minutes.
4. Add the fresh cream, mix well and cook for a minute.
5. Halve the eggs vertically and add to the gravy. Mix gently and simmer for two minutes.
6. Serve hot.

Calories: 235.25

Carbohydrates: 17.8

Protein: 11.1

Fat: 13.32

Fibre: 1.9

Iron: 2.62

Folic Acid: 55.5

RICE, NOODLES AND PASTA

GREEN MANGO AND PEANUT RICE

It is not for nothing that mango is called the king of fruits – it is not just tasty it is extremely rich in essential nutrients. This combination of unripe mango, peanuts and rice is simply irresistible.

Ingredients

- 1½ cups rice, soaked for ½ hour
- 110 grams green (unripe) mango, grated coarsely
- ½ cup raw peanuts
- Salt to taste
- 3 tablespoons pure ghee
- 1 teaspoon mustard seeds
- A pinch of asafoetida
- 2 dried red chillies, broken
- 1 tablespoon skinless split black gram
- 1 tablespoon split Bengal gram
- 10-12 curry leaves
- ½ teaspoon turmeric powder
- 2 tablespoons chopped fresh coriander

Method

1. Drain the rice and cook in four cups of boiling salted water until almost done. Drain and set aside.
2. Heat the ghee in a non-stick kadai, add the peanuts and sauté till golden brown. Drain on absorbent paper and set aside.
3. In the same pan, add the mustard seeds and once they splutter, add the asafoetida, chillies, black gram and Bengal gram. Cook till the two dals change colour to light brown.
4. Add the curry leaves and turmeric powder and sauté for a few seconds.
5. Add the cooked rice, mango, peanuts and salt. Mix well, cover and cook on low heat for about five minutes.
6. Garnish with the chopped coriander and serve hot.

Calories: 541.125, **Carbohydrates:** 72.15, **Protein:** 13.27, **Fat:** 21.88
Fibre: 0.54, **Iron:** 3.607, **Folic Acid:** 10.46

ANDA PARANTHA

Nutrient dense eggs are undoubtedly one of the most nutritious foods for a pregnant woman. Only make sure they are properly cooked in order to prevent any bacterial infections.

Ingredients

- 5 eggs (ande)
- 1 cup refined flour
- 1 cup wholewheat flour + for dusting
- Salt to taste
- 2 green chillies, finely chopped
- ½ teaspoon carom seeds
- 3 teaspoons oil
- 2 tablespoons chopped fresh coriander

Method

1. Sift the flours with little salt into a bowl.
2. Break four eggs into another bowl, add salt and whisk.
3. Add the green chillies, carom seeds, one egg and approximately three-fourth cup water to the mixed flours and knead into a soft dough. Cover with a damp cloth and rest for an hour.
4. Divide the dough into four equal portions. Roll out each into a four-inch round disc. Apply one-fourth teaspoon oil on each disc, sprinkle a little wheat flour and fold into four.
5. Roll out again on floured surface into six-inch round parantha.
6. Heat a non-stick tawa; place a parantha on it. When the underside is half done, turn it over and spread some egg and sprinkle a little chopped coriander. Pour one-fourth teaspoon oil around the edges and turn it over. Spread some egg and sprinkle a little chopped coriander on the other side too. Drizzle one-fourth teaspoon oil and cook till both sides are evenly golden brown.
7. Serve hot.

Calories: 340, **Carbohydrates:** 48.25, **Protein:** 5.925, **Fat:** 9, **Fibre:** 0.7, **Iron:** 4.08, **Folic Acid:** 62.36

HARE PYAAZ AUR ALOO KA PARANTHA

Pregnant women do like to have variety of dishes and this is just one of them. Besides it is healthy and tasty too!

Ingredients

5-6 spring onions with greens (hare pyaaz), finely chopped

4 medium potatoes (aloo), boiled and mashed

1½ cups whole-wheat flour + for dusting

½ teaspoon carom seeds, crushed

Salt to taste

¼ cup yogurt

1 tablespoon oil

4 green chillies, chopped

2 teaspoons red chilli powder

4 tablespoons chopped fresh coriander

8 teaspoons pure ghee

Method

1. Place the flour in a deep bowl; add the carom seeds, spring onion with greens, salt and yogurt and knead into a soft dough. Apply the oil, cover with a damp cloth and rest for fifteen minutes.
2. To make the stuffing, mix the potatoes, green chillies, salt, chilli powder and chopped coriander in a bowl.
3. Divide the dough into eight equal portions and roll into balls. Shape each ball into a katori, place a spoonful of the stuffing in it, bring in the edges and shape them again into balls. Dust them with dry flour and roll into medium thick paranthe.
4. Heat a non-stick tawa and place a parantha on it. Cook on medium heat for two minutes. Turn it over and apply half teaspoon ghee on it, turn it over again and apply half teaspoon ghee on the other side too. Cook, turning sides, till both the sides turn golden brown.
5. Serve hot.

Calories: 468

Carbohydrates: 73.375

Protein: 7.75

Fat: 15.85

Fibre: 1.65

Iron: 4.281

Folic Acid: 46.96

BARBECUED CHICKEN LASAGNE

Feel like having something different from the daily fare of dal-roti-subzi-chawal, try this one - wholesome and completely satiating!

Ingredients

2 boneless chicken breasts, halved
10-12 lasagne sheets
4 tablespoons olive oil
Salt to taste
6-7 garlic cloves, crushed
2 teaspoons dark soy sauce
1 medium onion, chopped
2 inch celery stalk, chopped
2 cups Tomato Concassé (page 124)
½ cup tomato purée
½ teaspoon freshly ground black peppercorns
1 cup White Sauce (page 124)
15-20 fresh basil
½ cup grated cheese

Calories: 1024.75
Carbohydrates: 121.55
Protein: 40.52
Fat: 42.3
Fibre: 2.88
Iron: 5.13
Folic Acid: 1.5

Method

1. Boil plenty of water in a large deep non-stick pan. Add one tablespoon olive oil and when the water begins to boil, add the lasagne sheets and cook till al dente (cooked but firm to the bite). Drain and refresh in cold water. Drain and set aside to cool.
2. Preheat the oven to 180°C/350°F/Gas Mark 4.
3. Add the salt, half the garlic, dark soy sauce and one tablespoon olive oil to the chicken and marinate for fifteen minutes.
4. To make the sauce, heat one tablespoon olive oil in a non-stick pan; add the onion and remaining garlic and mix. Add the celery and mix. Add the tomato concassé and mix well.
5. Place the chicken on a non-stick grill pan and roast, basting with remaining olive oil and turning sides, till both sides are well cooked and evenly browned. Cut into cubes.
6. Add the tomato pureé to the sauce and mix. Add salt, freshly ground peppercorns and mix. Set the sauce aside.
7. Spread a little white sauce at the base of a large rectangular baking dish. Place a lasagne sheet, spread some of the tomato sauce over it. Sprinkle a few fresh basil leaves. Cover with another lasagne sheet. Spread a little white sauce and place some chicken cubes. Spread some tomato sauce, cover with another lasagne sheet. Make more layers in this manner till all the lasagne sheets, white sauce, tomato sauce and chicken cubes are used up. Make sure the topmost layer is of tomato sauce. Sprinkle the grated cheese evenly and place the remaining fresh basil. Bake in the preheated oven for twenty minutes.
8. Serve hot.

BROWN RICE WITH CHICKEN AND CINNAMON

Powerhouse of nutrients, packed with minerals and vitamins, brown rice is extremely good for an expectant mother.

Ingredients

- 1½ cups brown Basmati rice, soaked and drained
- 300 grams chicken, cut into 1-inch cubes on the bone
- 2 inches cinnamon
- 2 tablespoons ghee
- 2 star anise
- 6-8 cloves
- 2 large onions, sliced
- 2 teaspoons sugar
- Salt to taste

Method

1. Heat the ghee in a deep non-stick pan. Add the cinnamon, star anise and cloves and sauté for thirty seconds. Add the onions and sauté for seven to eight minutes or till well browned.
2. Add the sugar and sauté till it dissolves. Add the rice and mix.
3. Add eight cups of water and salt and bring it to a boil.
4. Lower the heat, cover and cook on medium heat for twenty to twenty-five minutes or till three-fourth done.
5. Add the chicken and mix well. Cook till the chicken is fully done.
6. Serve hot.

Calories: 418.25
Carbohydrates: 67.05
Protein: 18.7
Fat: 8.175
Fibre: 0.48
Iron: 4.281
Folic Acid: 6.7

JOWAR-BAJRE KI ROTI

Both jowar and bajra are considered body heating foods so make sure to serve these roti with plenty of fresh home-made butter or ghee.

Ingredients

¾ cup sorghum flour (jowar atta)

¾ cup millet flour (bajra atta)

½ cup whole-wheat flour + for dusting

Salt to taste

½ teaspoon green chilli paste

½ teaspoon cumin seeds

1 tablespoon chopped fresh coriander

4 teaspoons pure ghee

Yogurt, to serve

Method

1. Place all the three flours, salt, green chilli paste, cumin seeds and chopped coriander in a deep bowl and mix well. Knead into a medium stiff dough with three-fourth cup water. Add a tablespoon or two more water if required. Cover with a damp cloth and rest for five minutes.
2. Divide the dough into eight equal portions and shape into balls. Dust each ball with a little dry flour and roll out into a one-fourth inch thick roti.
3. Heat a non-stick tawa and cook the roti on it, turning sides, till both sides have golden flecks.
4. Take it off the heat, apply half teaspoon ghee and serve hot with yogurt.

Calories: 366.75

Carbohydrates: 46.15

Protein: 7.41

Fat: 16.887

Fibre: 0.995

Iron: 3.71

Folic Acid: 21.44

CHICKEN KEEMA PULAO

Whenever hunger pangs hit you and you feel like having something spicy and tasty, you can quickly dish up this pulao.

Ingredients

200 grams minced chicken (keema)
1½ cups Basmati rice, soaked
1½ inches ginger
10-12 garlic cloves
4 tablespoons oil
2 cloves
½ inch cinnamon
2 green cardamoms
8-10 black peppercorns
1 teaspoon cumin seeds
3 medium onions, sliced
3-4 green chillies, slit
1 teaspoon red chilli powder
2 medium tomatoes, chopped
Salt to taste
15-20 fresh mint, torn
2 tablespoons chopped fresh coriander
½ teaspoon Garam Masala Powder (page 123)

Method

1. Grind the ginger and garlic to a fine paste.
2. Heat the oil in a non-stick pan. Add the cloves, cinnamon, cardamoms, peppercorns, cumin seeds, onions and green chillies and sauté till the onions begin to change colour.
3. Add the minced chicken and cook on high heat for four to five minutes.
4. Add the ginger-garlic paste, chilli powder, tomatoes, three cups of hot water, salt and rice and mix lightly.
5. Allow the mixture to come to a boil on high heat. Cover the pan and cook on low heat for twelve to fifteen minutes.
6. Add the torn mint, chopped coriander and garam masala powder. Cover and cook further for five to seven minutes.
7. Take the pan off the heat and serve hot.

Calories: 495.25
Carbohydrates: 68.5
Protein: 19.375
Fat: 15.67
Fibre: 0.975
Iron: 3.165
Folic Acid: 7.9

KOKI

Don't let its simplicity mislead you – it's simply scrumptious and wholesome too!

Ingredients

- 2½ cups wholewheat flour
- 2 small onions, chopped
- Salt to taste
- 2-3 green chillies, finely chopped
- 2 tablespoons chopped fresh coriander
- 3-4 tablespoons pure ghee
- 4 tablespoons fresh cream

Method

1. Mix together the flour, onions, salt, green chillies, chopped coriander, one tablespoon ghee and cream in a deep bowl. Add enough water to make a stiff dough. Cover and rest the dough for about fifteen minutes.
2. Divide the dough into eight equal portions and shape into balls. Place each ball on a board. Pat lightly with your fingers into a thick round koki.
3. Heat a non-stick tawa; place a koki on it and cook. Turn over, drizzle a little ghee all around and turn over again. Drizzle a little ghee all around again, and cook till both sides are light golden in colour.
4. Best served hot.

Calories: 468.1
Carbohydrates: 69.75
Protein: 11.75
Fat: 15.31
Fibre: 1.75
Iron: 5.297
Folic Acid: 33.5

CURD RICE

Not only is yogurt a good source of protein, it also has more calcium than milk besides containing active cultures that reduce the risk of yeast infections, which are quite common amongst expectant women.

Ingredients

- 1 cup yogurt (curd)
- 1½ cups Kolam rice, soaked
- ½ cup milk
- Salt to taste
- 2 tablespoons oil
- 1 teaspoon mustard seeds
- ¼ teaspoon asafoetida
- 1 dried red chilli, broken
- 8-10 curry leaves
- 1 inch ginger, chopped
- 4 green chillies, chopped
- ¼ cup fresh cream
- 1 medium cucumber, peeled, seeded and grated
- 1 medium carrot, grated

Method

1. Drain and boil the rice in four and a half cups of water till it is slightly overcooked. Drain well and cool. When it reaches room temperature, add the milk and salt.
2. Heat the oil in a small non-stick pan; add the mustard seeds, asafoetida, dried chilli and curry leaves. When the seeds begin to splutter, add the ginger and green chillies and sauté for half a minute. Add the seasoning to the rice.
3. Add the yogurt and cream. Mix well and transfer into a bowl and chill in the refrigerator.
4. Squeeze out excess water from the cucumber. Garnish the rice with the cucumber and carrot and serve chilled.

Chef's Tip: If you are preparing the recipe well in advance, reduce the quantity of yogurt and increase the quantity of milk. This will prevent the rice from becoming too sour.

Calories: 425.25
Carbohydrates: 63.345
Protein: 7.83
Fat: 16.9
Fibre: 0.35
Iron: 2.845
Folic Acid: 9.68

MUSHROOM DUM BIRYANI

This is just the recipe to pamper your loved ones – especially if the person is in the family way. It's a bit lengthy, but the end result is well worth all that effort.

Ingredients

15-20 fresh button mushrooms, quartered, •1½ cups Basmati rice, soaked, •1 bay leaf •4 cloves •2 green cardamoms •2 black cardamoms •1 inch cinnamon •1 blade mace •Salt to taste •A generous pinch of saffron •¼ cup warm skimmed milk •2 teaspoons oil •2 medium onions, finely sliced •1 teaspoon fresh ginger paste •1 teaspoon fresh garlic paste •2 teaspoons red chilli powder •1 tablespoon coriander powder •10-12 black peppercorns, crushed •½ teaspoon roasted cumin powder •½ teaspoon turmeric powder •2 medium tomatoes, puréed •½ cup skimmed milk yogurt, whisked •½ teaspoon Garam Masala powder (page 123) •¼ cup chopped fresh coriander •¼ cup fresh mint, roughly torn •4-5 drops screw pine essence (optional)

Method

1. Bring four cups of water to a boil in a thick-bottomed non-stick pan. Add the bay leaf, cloves, green cardamoms, black cardamoms, cinnamon, mace and one teaspoon salt. When the water starts boiling vigorously, add the drained rice.
2. Cook for eight to ten minutes, or until the rice is three-fourth done, stirring frequently. Drain in a colander.
3. Soak the saffron in the milk.
4. Heat the oil in a non-stick pan; add the sliced onions and sauté over high heat for two to three minutes, or until translucent. Add the ginger paste and garlic paste, and sauté for a few seconds.
5. Add the chilli powder, coriander powder, crushed peppercorns, cumin powder and turmeric powder. Sauté for a few seconds and add the puréed tomatoes.
6. Continue cooking over high heat for further two or three minutes, or until the masala is fairly thick, stirring continuously.
7. Add the yogurt, garam masala powder and half the fresh coriander and mint leaves. Stir well and cook for two minutes longer.
8. Add the mushrooms and salt to taste. Sauté over high heat for two or three minutes and remove from heat.
9. Arrange the cooked rice and mushroom masala in alternate layers in an oven-proof dish (or Biryani handi), sprinkling the remaining chopped fresh coriander and mint leaves, screw pine essence and saffron-flavoured milk over each layer. The top-most layer should be rice.
10. Cover the assembled biryani with a tight-fitting lid and seal the edges with atta (dough).
11. Place the sealed handi on a medium hot tawa and leave for ten to fifteen minutes. You can also place a few burning charcoals on the lid. Alternatively, place the sealed dish in a preheated oven and cook at 200°C/400°F/Gas Mark 6 for ten to fifteen minutes.
12. Break the seal and uncover the dish, just before serving.

Calories: 348.1 **Carbohydrates:** 67.64 **Protein:** 8.54 **Fat:** 5.5 **Fibre:** 1.47
Iron: 3.35 **Folic Acid:** 13.81

FADA NI KHICHDI

Broken wheat with its high fibre content will relieve constipation which troubles quite a few pregnant women.

Ingredients

½ cup broken wheat (fada/dalia), soaked for 15 minutes
3 tablespoons pure ghee
1 inch cinnamon
2 cloves
1 teaspoon cumin seeds
¼ teaspoon asafoetida
¼ cup skinless split green gram, soaked for 15 minutes
Salt to taste
½ teaspoon turmeric powder
1 teaspoon ginger-green chilli paste
2 medium onions, chopped
2 medium tomatoes, chopped
2 teaspoons Pav Bhaji Masala (page 123)
2 small potatoes, boiled, peeled and diced
½ cup shelled green peas, blanched

Method

1. Heat one tablespoon of ghee in a pressure cooker. Add the cinnamon, cloves, cumin seeds and asafoetida and sauté for thirty seconds.
2. Add the split green gram, broken wheat, salt and turmeric powder and mix. Add four cups of water and close the lid of the cooker and cook till pressure is released three to four times (three to four whistles).
3. Open the lid when the pressure reduces completely.
4. Heat the remaining ghee in a deep non-stick pan. Add the ginger-green chilli paste and sauté for a minute.
5. Add the onions and sauté till translucent. Add the tomatoes and cook for four to five minutes.
6. Add salt and pav bhaji masala and cook till the oil separates from the masala.
7. Add the potatoes and green peas and cook for a few minutes. Add the boiled khichdi to the pan and cook for a minute.
8. Serve hot.

Calories: 311.5
Carbohydrates: 42.525
Protein: 7.975
Fat: 11.775
Fibre: 1.95
Iron: 2.52
Folic Acid: 17.12

PASTA WITH CHICKEN AND CHERRY TOMATOES

It is colourful, it is tasty and full of flavour and nutrients – what more can you ask for?

Ingredients

3 cups cooked farfalle pasta

200 grams boneless chicken, cut into thin strips

12 cherry tomatoes, halved

1 tablespoon olive oil

8-10 garlic cloves, chopped

1 teaspoon red chilli flakes

1 sprig fresh thyme

4 fresh button mushrooms, thickly sliced

Salt to taste

¼ teaspoon crushed black peppercorns

½ cup fresh cream

1 cup milk

½ tablespoon Parmesan cheese

1 tablespoon chopped fresh parsley

Method

1. Heat the olive oil in a non-stick pan; add the garlic and sauté till golden brown.
2. Add the chilli flakes, chicken and thyme and sauté on high heat for two to three minutes.
3. Add the cherry tomatoes and mushrooms and cook for two to three minutes.
4. Add the pasta and toss well. Add the salt, crushed peppercorns, cream and milk and mix well.
5. Add the Parmesan cheese and mix well.
6. Serve hot garnished with the chopped parsley.

Calories: 300.75

Carbohydrates: 26.84

Protein: 19.91

Fat: 11.71

Fibre: 2.21

Iron: 0.74

Folic Acid: 34.2

FETTUCINE IN CREAMY PESTO SAUCE

Pine nuts are known to be powerhouse of useful nutrients and basil too is not far behind with vitamin A and K, folate and manganese – the combination of these two make this dish extremely healthy.

Ingredients

200 grams fresh fettuccine
1 teaspoon salt
1 tablespoon oil

Pesto Sauce

30-40 (¾ cup) fresh basil
3-4 garlic cloves
Salt to taste
3 tablespoons pine nuts
6 tablespoons olive oil
4-5 black peppercorns
¼ cup Parmesan cheese

To Serve

2 tablespoons olive oil
Salt to taste
5-6 black peppercorns, crushed
½ cup milk
2 tablespoons Parmesan cheese
3-4 fresh basil

Method

1. To make the pesto sauce, blend together the fresh basil, garlic and salt for a few seconds. Add the pine nuts, olive oil, peppercorns and Parmesan cheese, one by one, blending after each addition, till all the ingredients are well mixed. Transfer into a bowl.
2. Boil plenty of water with salt in a deep non-stick pan. Add one tablespoon oil and the fettucine and cook till al dente (cooked but firm to the bite).
3. Meanwhile, heat two tablespoons olive oil in another non-stick pan; add the pesto sauce and sauté for four to five minutes.
4. Drain the fettucine and add to the pesto. Toss well so that the sauce coats the pasta.
5. Stir in salt and freshly crushed peppercorns. Add milk and Parmesan cheese and mix well. Tear the fresh basil and add to the pasta. Toss once again.
6. Serve immediately.

Calories: 570.5, **Carbohydrates:** 38.375, **Protein:** 9.55, **Fat:** 41.5, **Iron:** 0.65, **Folic Acid:** 6

SPINACH, MUSHROOM AND EGG FRIED RICE

When the mother-to-be is feeling low, perk her up with this dish - it has this feel good effect.

Ingredients

- 2 cups cooked rice
- 10-12 fresh spinach leaves, shredded
- 10-12 fresh button mushrooms, sliced
- 2 eggs, beaten
- 2 tablespoons + 2 teaspoons oil
- 8-10 garlic cloves, chopped
- 1 inch ginger, finely chopped
- 1 green chilli, chopped
- 1 tablespoon soy sauce
- 3 teaspoons chilli sauce
- Salt to taste
- 2 teaspoons vinegar
- 2 tablespoons chopped spring onion greens

Method

1. Heat two tablespoons oil in a non-stick wok; add the garlic, ginger and green chilli and sauté for a minute.
2. Add the mushrooms and cook till soft. Add the soy sauce and chilli sauce and mix well.
3. Add the cooked rice and salt. Toss well. Add the spinach leaves and cook for a minute.
4. Heat two teaspoons oil in another non-stick pan. Add the beaten eggs and cook, stirring, till set and scrambled. Add to the rice and mix well. Add the vinegar and toss.
5. Serve hot garnished with spring onion greens.

Calories: 321

Carbohydrates: 39.71

Protein: 8.1

Fat: 14.18

Fibre: 0.775

Iron: 1.39

Folic Acid: 48.41

FIVE-SPICE NOODLES AND VEGETABLE STIR-FRY

Five-spice adds that special flavour to the noodles and vegetables that go into making this extremely delightful dish.

Ingredients

- 200 grams noodles, boiled
- 1 teaspoon five-spice powder
- 1 medium carrot, sliced
- 7-8 fresh button mushrooms, sliced
- 8-10 broccoli florets
- 8-10 French beans, cut diagonally into small pieces
- 1 tablespoon cornflour
- ½ cup orange juice
- 2 tablespoons oil
- 5-6 garlic cloves, chopped
- 1 medium onion, sliced
- Salt to taste
- 2 tablespoons soy sauce
- 1 teaspoon crushed red chillies

Method

1. Mix the cornflour with orange juice in a bowl and set aside.
2. Heat two tablespoons of oil in a non-stick wok; add the garlic, carrot and mushrooms and stir-fry for thirty seconds.
3. Add the onion, broccoli, French beans, salt, soy sauce, one-fourth teaspoon crushed chillies and five-spice powder and continue to stir-fry for three to four minutes.
4. Add the cornflour mixture and one cup of water. Stir and cook till the mixture thickens.
5. Add the noodles and toss well. Serve hot.

Calories: 351.25, **Carbohydrates:** 46.49, **Protein:** 6.3, **Fat:** 15.32, **Fibre:** 0.995 **Iron:** 2.037, **Folic Acid:** 29.1

ACCOMPANIMENTS

AAMER CHAATNI

Sweet, sour and full of flavour, this was Alyona's favourite when we were expecting our first child, Rachita.

Ingredients

4 medium unripe mangoes (aam)
2 teaspoons oil
2 teaspoons Paanch Phoron (see below)
2 dried red chillies, broken
1 cup grated jaggery
Salt to taste

Method

1. Cut the unripe mangoes with the skin, into one-fourth inch thick slices. The seed too can be used, if desired.
2. Heat the oil in a non-stick pan. Add one teaspoon paanch phoron and the dried chillies. When the seeds begin to splutter; add the mango slices and sauté for a minute.
3. Add two cups of warm water and the mango seeds (if using) and mix.
4. Add the jaggery and cook, stirring continuously, on medium heat till the mangoes are cooked and the mixture thickens.
5. Remove the mango seeds and discard them. Add the salt and mix.
6. Roast the remaining paanch phoron on a non-stick tawa. Cool and grind to a powder.
7. When the chutney is cool, sprinkle this powder on top and serve.

Chef's Note: Paanch Phoron is a mixture of equal amounts of cumin seeds, fennel seeds, fenugreek seeds, mustard seeds and onion seeds.

Calories: 216
Carbohydrates: 53.1
Protein: 0.88
Fat: 0.1
Fibre: 1.2
Iron: 1.49

BEETROOT RAITA

Nutritionally rich beetroot is highly recommended for pregnant women because it contains folic acid that can help lower the risk of neural tube defects in newborn infants.

Ingredients

- 2 medium beetroots
- 3 cups yogurt
- 1 teaspoon roasted cumin powder
- 1 teaspoon red chilli powder
- Salt to taste

Method

1. Boil the beetroots in sufficient water till soft. Cool, peel and cut into one-fourth inch pieces. Set aside.
2. Beat the yogurt till smooth. You can also strain it through a piece of muslin.
3. Mix the beetroots with yogurt. Add the cumin powder, chilli powder and salt.
4. Mix well and serve chilled.

Chef's Tip: The bright and dark colour of beetroot will bleed and change the colour of the yogurt to a dark pink.

Calories: 133

Carbohydrates: 13.3

Protein: 6.35

Fat: 12

Fibre: 0.9

Iron: 1.15

Folic Acid: 15.99

AMLA MURABBA

Amla (Indian gooseberries) is considered to be the richest source of Vitamin C besides having considerable amounts of calcium, phosphorus and iron that a pregnant woman needs during pregnancy.

Ingredients

½ kg fresh Indian gooseberries (amla)

1 kg sugar

½ teaspoon green cardamom seeds, lightly crushed

½ teaspoon saffron threads, lightly crushed

Method

1. Place the Indian gooseberries in a deep non-stick pan and add two cups of water. Cover and cook on low heat for ten to fifteen minutes or till the gooseberries are tender and the water has reduced to half its original volume. Cool, remove the seeds and set aside.
2. Cook the sugar with six cups of water in another deep thick-bottomed non-stick pan, stirring continuously, till a sugar syrup of one-string consistency is formed.
3. Add the cooked gooseberries along with the cooking water and stir. Add the crushed green cardamom seeds and saffron and continue to cook, uncovered, on low heat till the mixture is thick and translucent. The syrup by now should be of two-string consistency.
4. Cool and store in airtight jars.

Calories: 1072.5

Carbohydrates: 267.1

Protein: 0.6

Fat: 0.1

Fibre: 4.02

Iron: 1.5

TOMATO CHUTNEY

Sweet and sour, with sesame seeds and peanuts adding a special dose of proteins, just the thing for an expectant mother to have in between meals.

Ingredients

- 4 large ripe red tomatoes, roughly chopped
- 3 teaspoons oil
- 3 inches ginger, finely chopped
- 1 medium onion, finely chopped
- 1 tablespoon sesame seeds, roasted and powdered
- 1 tablespoon peanuts, roasted and powdered
- 1 teaspoon roasted cumin seeds, powdered
- 2 teaspoons red chilli powder
- 1 tablespoon grated jaggery
- Salt to taste
- ½ teaspoon mustard seeds
- 10-12 curry leaves

Method

1. Heat two teaspoons oil in a deep non-stick pan. Add the tomatoes, ginger and onion. Stir and cook for twenty minutes or till the mixture becomes brown and homogenous.
2. Take the pan off the heat and set aside to cool.
3. Add the powdered sesame seeds, peanuts, cumin seeds, chilli powder, jaggery and salt and mix well. Transfer the mixture into a blender jar and blend into a smooth paste. Transfer into a bowl.
4. Heat the remaining oil in another non-stick pan. Add the mustard seeds and curry leaves. When the seeds begin to splutter add the seasoning to the chutney and stir.
5. Cool completely and store in an airtight bottle to use when required.

Calories: 123.25, **Carbohydrates:** 13.29, **Protein:** 2.61, **Fat:** 6.37, **Fibre:** 1.17, **Iron:** 1.42, **Folic Acid:** 40.02

ANGOOR AUR KHAJUR KI CHUTNEY

Grapes, dates and jaggery - all things nice that are good for the development of a healthy baby.

Ingredients

25-30 seedless grapes (angoor)

250 grams seedless dates (khajur), chopped

1 teaspoon red chilli powder

½ teaspoon roasted cumin powder

1½ tablespoons raisins

Salt to taste

¼ cup grated jaggery

Method

1. Cook the grapes and dates in a deep non-stick pan with two to three tablespoons of water, on medium heat, till the grapes are completely soft and mashed.
2. Add the chilli powder, cumin powder and raisins and cook for five minutes.
3. Add the salt and jaggery and mix well. Cook, stirring continuously, till the jaggery is completely dissolved and well blended.
4. Serve at room temperature.

Calories: 162

Carbohydrates: 38.72

Protein: 0.99

Fat: 0.32

Fibre: 3.03

Iron: 1.02

CUCUMBER RAITA WITH FLAX SEEDS

Flaxseeds are rich in omega-3-fatty acids, fibre, B vitamins, minerals like magnesium and manganese – all things that are necessary for healthy growth. Just the kind of food an expectant mother should have.

Ingredients

2 medium cucumbers, peeled and grated

4 tablespoons roasted flax seeds

1 cup yogurt, whisked

½ teaspoon roasted cumin powder

Salt to taste

A pinch of Kashmiri red chilli powder

2 tablespoons chopped fresh coriander

Method

1. Place the cucumbers, yogurt, roasted cumin powder, salt, chilli powder and chopped coriander in a bowl and mix well. Chill in the refrigerator.
2. Transfer into individual serving bowls and sprinkle with the flax seeds.
3. Serve chilled.

Calories: 101.75

Carbohydrates: 6.1

Protein: 3.8

Fat: 9.27

Fibre: 3.45

Iron: 11.16

Folic Acid: 6.04

TOMATO RASAM

Lot of women crave for tangy foods during pregnancy and this rasam is just right for that. Besides tomatoes have adequate vitamins and minerals necessary for a pregnant woman.

Ingredients

2 medium tomatoes, chopped

4 tablespoons split pigeon peas, soaked for 30 minutes

¾ teaspoon turmeric powder

2½ tablespoons Tamarind Pulp (page 123)

Salt to taste

1½ teaspoons Rasam Powder (page 124)

¼ teaspoon asafoetida

4 tablespoons chopped fresh coriander

2 tablespoons pure ghee

½ teaspoon mustard seeds

½ teaspoon cumin seeds

5-6 curry leaves

¼ teaspoon black pepper powder

Method

1. Boil four-and-a-half cups of water in a deep non-stick pan on high heat. Add half the turmeric powder and drained split pigeon peas. Lower heat to medium and cook for fifteen minutes or until soft. Strain and use the stock only.
2. Heat the tamarind pulp, two-and-a-half cups of water, tomatoes, salt, remaining turmeric powder, rasam powder and half the asafoetida in another deep non-stick pan. Once the mixture comes to a boil, lower the heat to medium and simmer for ten to fifteen minutes or till it reduces to half its original volume.
3. Add the strained stock and chopped coriander and continue to boil for three to five minutes more. Take the pan off the heat.
4. For the seasoning, heat the ghee in a small non-stick pan and add the mustard seeds and cumin seeds. When they begin to splutter add the curry leaves, remaining asafoetida and pepper powder.
5. Add the seasoning to the rasam and cover immediately to trap the flavours.
6. Serve hot with steamed rice.

Calories: 137

Carbohydrates: 11.67

Protein: 3.75

Fat: 8.4

Fibre: 0.57

Iron: 0.74

Folic Acid: 31.24

SWEETS AND DESSERTS

ANJEER AUR KHAJUR KI BURFI

Figs are rich in fibre and ideal to avoid constipation. Dates are rich in iron which is necessary to build up haemoglobin – this combination is ideal for a pregnant woman.

Ingredients

- 20-25 dried figs (anjeer)
- 1½ cups seedless dates (khajur), chopped
- ¼ cup ghee
- 25-30 almonds, finely chopped
- 15-20 cashew nuts, finely chopped
- 15-20 pistachios, finely chopped
- 1-2 sheets edible silver foil

Method

1. Soak the figs in two cups of water for three to four hours. Drain and purée, adding a little water if required. Alternatively, place the figs in one cup of hot water for two to three minutes. Drain and cool. Make a purée, adding a little water if required.
2. Heat the ghee in a non-stick pan; add the fig purée and dates and mix well. Cook on medium heat, stirring continuously, for ten to fifteen minutes or till excess moisture dries up.
3. Add the almonds, cashew nuts and pistachios. Mix well and continue to cook, stirring continuously, for ten to fifteen minutes or till the mixture begins to leave the sides of the pan.
4. Spread evenly on a greased tray. Cover with silver varq.
5. When cool, cut into pieces and serve.

Chef's Tip: By adding just five or six fresh figs to your morning bowl of cereal you'll be eating over half your recommended daily allowance of fibre in one easy go while dates are a very good source of iron.

Calories: 453, **Carbohydrates:** 69.3, **Protein:** 5.37, **Fat:** 25.55, **Fibre:** 9.62, **Iron:** 3.3, **Folic Acid:** 13.95

BLACK CURRANT ICE CREAM

The presence of health benefiting phytonutrients and antioxidants in black currants make them very beneficial for consumption. However pregnant women should consume this berry in moderation.

Ingredients

½ cup black currant crush

1 cup chilled milk

1 cup chilled fresh cream

1 cup milk powder

Method

1. Pour the milk into a blender jar; add the fresh cream, milk powder and black currant crush and blend well.
2. Pour into an ice cream container and freeze till well set.
3. Slice and serve.

Calories: 203.75

Carbohydrates: 18.3

Protein: 7.85

Fat: 10.3

Iron: 0.4

Folic Acid: 4.25

APPLE RABDI

Apples are good source of vitamin C, pectin, soluble and insoluble fibre, flavonoids and antioxidants - are these not enough reason to consume this wonder fruit?

Ingredients

3 medium apples

1 litre milk

4 tablespoons sugar

¼ teaspoon green cardamom powder

8-10 almonds, blanched and sliced

8-10 pistachios, blanched and sliced

Method

1. Pour the milk into a wide non-stick pan and bring to a boil. Simmer till reduced to half the original quantity.
2. Add the sugar and cook on low heat, stirring continuously.
3. Peel and grate two apples and add to the reduced milk and mix. Cook for three to four minutes. Add the cardamom powder, almonds and pistachios and mix well.
4. Pour into a serving bowl. Thinly slice the remaining apple and arrange them all around the dish.
5. Serve hot or cold.

Calories: 308.875

Carbohydrates: 38.57

Protein: 9.06

Fat: 13.49

Fibre: 0.94

Iron: 1.3

Folic Acid: 21.25

BROWN BREAD AND BUTTER PUDDING WITH PLUM COMPOTE

Just two slices of brown bread daily can stave off high blood pressure in pregnant women.

Ingredients

6 brown bread slices
3 tablespoons butter
2 cups milk
½ cup sugar
2 eggs
1 teaspoon vanilla essence
½ cup raisins

Plum compote

5 plums, seeded and chopped
½ cup sugar
1 tablespoon butter

Method

1. Preheat an oven to 180°C/350°F/Gas Mark 4.
2. Trim off the crusts of the bread slices and apply butter only on one side. Cut the slices into triangles. Arrange the triangles in a baking dish with the buttered side up.
3. Heat the milk in a non-stick pan, add the sugar and stir till the sugar dissolves.
4. Break the eggs in a bowl but do not beat them. Add the eggs to the milk and mix. Add the vanilla essence.
5. Sprinkle the raisins over the bread pieces and pour the egg-milk mixture over them through a strainer. Bake in the preheated oven for twenty-five to thirty minutes.
6. To make the plum compote, mix the sugar and plums in a non-stick pan and cook till the plums become soft and pulpy.
7. Take the pan off the heat and add the butter and mix well.
8. Serve the pudding hot or cold topped with the plum compote.

Calories: 648.5
Carbohydrates: 118.25
Protein: 9.2
Fat: 14.91
Fibre: 1.65
Iron: 3.57
Folic Acid: 32.12

BADAMI SHEERA

Packed with minerals like calcium and phosphorus that contribute to strong bones and dental health, almonds are indeed a very good snack for women who are expecting or breastfeeding.

Ingredients

½ cup almonds (badam), blanched and peeled

½ cup semolina

3 tablespoons ghee

2 cups milk

⅓ cup sugar

¼ teaspoon green cardamom powder

Method

1. Sliver three to four almonds for garnishing and grind the rest coarsely.
2. Heat the ghee in a non-stick kadai; add the semolina and sauté on low heat, stirring continuously, till it begins to change colour. Add the ground almonds and continue to sauté till the mixture turns golden brown.
3. Boil the milk with one cup of water in a deep non-stick pan and add to the semolina mixture. Cook, stirring continuously, for two minutes.
4. Add the sugar and cardamom powder and continue to cook, stirring continuously, till the sugar dissolves completely.
5. Serve hot garnished with the almond slivers.

Calories: 419.75

Carbohydrates: 45.2

Protein: 8.9

Fat: 22.6

Fibre: 0.37

Iron: 1.55

Folic Acid: 8.5

CARAMEL CUSTARD

Combination of milk and eggs, being rich in proteins and calcium, is very beneficial for a pregnant woman.

Ingredients

2½ cups milk

5 eggs

1½ cups caster sugar

A few drops of vanilla essence

Method

1. Preheat an oven to 180°C/350°F/Gas Mark 4.
2. Pour the milk into a deep non-stick pan and bring to a boil. Take it off the heat and set aside.
3. Break the eggs into a bowl; add three-fourth of the caster sugar and vanilla essence and beat till well blended. Add the milk slowly to the egg mixture and mix well.
4. Put the remaining caster sugar in a non-stick pan; add one tablespoon water and heat till the sugar melts and caramelises. Once it becomes light golden in colour, pour it carefully into ramekin moulds and allow it to set.
5. Pour the custard mixture into the moulds. Arrange them in a baking tray; pour some water in the tray till it reaches half way up the moulds and place the tray in the preheated oven. Bake for forty to forty-five minutes.
6. Remove the moulds from the oven and let them cool down to room temperature. Refrigerate for one to two hours.
7. Remove custard from the moulds and serve.

Calories: 434.5

Carbohydrates: 51.25

Protein: 13.37

Fat: 16.1

Iron: 1.56

Folic Acid: 59.6

BAKED MANGO CHEESECAKE

Make the most of the mango season with this delightful dish. It tastes as good as it looks and what's more it is full of nutrients too.

Ingredients

½ cup ripe mango pulp
2 tablespoons mango jelly crystals
250 grams cream cheese
8 digestive biscuits, crushed
50 grams unsalted butter, melted
3 eggs
80 grams caster sugar

Method

1. Place the crushed biscuits in a bowl; add the melted butter and mix.
2. Line the base of a spring-form cake tin evenly with this mixture. Press lightly and place the tin in the refrigerator to chill for thirty minutes.
3. Preheat an oven to 180°C/350°F/Gas Mark 4.
4. Break the eggs into a bowl; add the sugar and mix with a hand blender till frothy.
5. Place the cream cheese in another bowl; add the mango pulp and mix with a hand blender. Add the egg mixture and mix. Pour this mixture over the biscuit base.
6. Place the tin in the preheated oven and bake for about forty minutes or till well set.
7. Take it out of the oven and cool to room temperature. Place it in the refrigerator to chill.
8. Heat half a cup of water in a small non-stick pan, add the mango jelly crystals and mix till well dissolved. Take the pan off the heat and cool to room temperature. Pour the mixture carefully over the chilled cheesecake and place it in the refrigerator till the jelly sets.
9. Just before serving, remove the tin from the refrigerator and open the spring-form tin to release the cheesecake. Place it on a serving plate, cut into wedges and serve.

Calories: 627.75

Carbohydrates: 47.025

Protein: 10.8

Fat: 43.15

Fibre: 1.47

Iron: 1.11

Folic Acid: 29.025

CHOCOLATE CHIP AND OAT COOKIES

Eating moderate amounts of chocolate during pregnancy is perfectly safe. And when combined with oats, which is considered beneficial especially since it has considerable amounts of folic acid and iron which are nutrients crucial during prenatal period.

Ingredients

- ¼ cup dark chocolate chips
- 1 cup rolled oats
- ⅔ cup wholewheat flour
- ½ teaspoon baking powder
- ¾ cup butter, softened
- 4 tablespoons brown sugar
- 1 teaspoon vanilla essence

Method

1. Preheat an oven to 180°C/350°F/Gas Mark 4.
2. Sift together wholewheat flour and baking powder in a bowl. Add the chocolate chips and rolled oats and mix well.
3. In another bowl, cream the butter and brown sugar till fluffy. Add the vanilla essence and mix well. Fold in the flour mixture and mix well.
4. Divide the dough into equal portions and flatten between your palms to make thick cookies.
5. Place the cookies on a baking tray, keeping some distance between each, and bake in the preheated oven for twenty-five to thirty minutes or till the cookies turn golden brown.
6. Cool completely and store in an air-tight container.

Calories: 512.75

Carbohydrates: 85.2

Protein: 5.97

Fat: 16.67

Fibre: 2.37

Iron: 2.07

Folic Acid: 15.45

BANANA AND WALNUT MUFFINS

Bananas are rich in potassium which can make one feel energised and maintain fluid and electrolyte balance in the body's cells. And walnuts provide proteins and omega-3 fats which are good for the development of the baby's brain and eyes. So all in all these muffins are very good for the expectant mother.

Ingredients

¾ cup banana purée

½ cup chopped walnuts

2 cups refined flour + for dusting

1 teaspoon baking powder

¼ cup dark chocolate chips

¼ cup rolled oats

2 cups butter

2 cups brown sugar

5 eggs

A few drops of vanilla essence

Method

1. Preheat an oven to 180°C/350°F/Gas Mark 4.
2. Sift together the flour and baking powder into a bowl. Add the chocolate chips and rolled oats and mix well.
3. Cream the butter and sugar till light and fluffy and gradually add the eggs, two or three at a time, and whisk till the mixture is light. Add the vanilla essence, banana purée and mix well. Fold in the flour mixture into this.
4. Dust half the walnuts with flour and fold the walnuts into the batter.
5. Pipe the mixture into silicon muffin moulds. Sprinkle the remaining walnuts on top of the muffins. Place the moulds in the preheated oven and bake for twenty to twenty-five minutes.
6. Remove from moulds and serve.

Calories: 1688.5

Carbohydrates: 181.6

Protein: 17.86

Fat: 99.45

Fibre: 1.55

Iron: 3.59

Folic Acid: 50.6

GAUR PAPDI

Jaggery is a very good source of iron and therefore apt for a pregnant woman.

Ingredients

- ¾ cup finely chopped jaggery (gaur/gur)
- 1 cup wholewheat flour
- 1 teaspoon poppy seeds
- 5 tablespoons pure ghee + for greasing
- ¼ teaspoon green cardamom powder
- 1 teaspoon desiccated coconut

Method

1. Sprinkle the poppy seeds on a greased thali and set aside.
2. Heat the ghee in a non-stick pan; add the flour and sauté, stirring continuously, till it turns golden brown. Take the pan off the heat and let it cool for thirty seconds.
3. Add the jaggery, cardamom powder and desiccated coconut. Mix till the jaggery melts.
4. Pour the mixture into the thali and spread evenly. Cut into desired shapes while still warm and set aside to cool completely.
5. Separate the pieces and store in an air-tight container.

Calories: 330.25

Carbohydrates: 32.1

Protein: 4.72

Fat: 19.55

Fibre: 0.7

Iron: 2.1

Folic Acid: 13.4

ANNEXURE

CHAAT MASALA

Dry roast 4 tablespoons coriander seeds, 2 teaspoons cumin seeds and 1 teaspoon carom seeds (ajwain) separately. Cool and powder them with 2-3 whole dry red chillies, 3 tablespoons black salt and ½ teaspoon citric acid. Mix in 1 teaspoon dry mango powder (amchur), 1 tablespoon salt and 1 teaspoon white/black pepper powder. Store in an airtight container.

CHICKEN STOCK

Boil 200 grams chicken bones in 2 cups of water for 5 minutes. Drain the water. Add 1 medium quartered onion, 1 medium roughly chopped carrot, 1 stalk of celery, 2-3 stalks of parsley, 1 leek with leaves, 6-7 peppercorns, 5-6 cloves, 1 bay leaf and 10 cups of water and bring the mixture to a boil. Reduce the heat, remove any scum that may rise to the top and replace it with more cold water. Simmer the stock for a minimum period of 1 hour. Strain, cool and store in a refrigerator till further use.

GARAM MASALA POWDER

Lightly dry roast 10-12 blades of mace, 8-10 one inch sticks of cinnamon, 25 cloves, 25 green cardamoms, 10-12 black cardamoms, 2 nutmegs, 8-10 bay leaves, 8 teaspoons cumin seeds, 4 teaspoons black peppercorns one by one. Cool and grind to a fine powder. (Makes 100 grams of garam masala powder)

GREEN CHUTNEY

Grind 1 cup fresh coriander, ½ cup fresh mint and 2-3 green chillies to a smooth paste with a little water if required. Add the black salt and ¼ teaspoon sugar. Transfer the chutney into a bowl, add 1 teaspoon lemon juice, and mix well.

VEGETABLE STOCK

Boil 5 cups of water with 1 medium sliced onion, ½ medium sliced carrot, 3 inch chopped celery stalk, 2 garlic cloves, 1 bay leaf, 5-6 black peppercorns and 2-3 cloves. Reduce the heat and simmer for 30 minutes. Strain the stock into a bowl and set aside to cool. Store in a refrigerator till further use.

TAMARIND PULP

Soak 75 grams tamarind in 100 ml warm water for 10-15 minutes. Grind to a smooth paste and strain to remove any fibres. Store in an airtight container in the refrigerator.

ANNEXURE

MAYONNAISE

Place 1 egg yolk, salt, ¼ teaspoon white pepper powder, ¼ teaspoon French mustard powder, ¼ teaspoon sugar and 1 teaspoon vinegar in a clean bowl. Whisk thoroughly with a whisk or else transfer into a blender and blend. Add 1 cup oil, a little at a time, whisking/blending continuously, until all the oil is incorporated. Add 1 teaspoon lemon juice and adjust the seasoning.

PAV BHAJI MASALA

Dry roast 1½ tablespoons dried mango powder (amchur), ½ teaspoon black peppercorns, 12 Kashmiri dried red chillies, 2 tablespoons cumin seeds, 2½ tablespoons coriander seeds, 6 one-inch cinnamon sticks, 1 tablespoon salt, ¼ teaspoon black salt, 25 cloves, 1 black cardamom, 6-8 curry leaves, 2 bay leaves and 1 tablespoon fennel seeds (saunf) in a small non-stick pan on medium heat for 5 minutes. Cool completely and grind to a smooth powder. Store in an airtight container.

RASAM POWDER

Dry roast 1 cup coriander seeds, ½ cup split pigeon pea, 4 tablespoons cumin seeds, 4 tablespoons black peppercorns, 12 curry leaves and 15 dried red chillies for 3-4 minutes or until fragrant. Cool and grind into a fine powder. When the powder is completely cooled, transfer into air tight jars and use as required. You can store it in a refrigerator or in cool, dry place for upto 6 months.

WHITE SAUCE

Melt 1½ tablespoons butter in a non-stick pan, add 1½ cups refined flour, stir and cook the roux (butter-flour mixture) over low heat with a wooden spoon. When it gets the sandy texture, remove from the heat and cool. Wrap 1 bay leaf around 1 medium onion, fix it with 1 cloves at each end. Heat 1½ cups milk in another non stick pan, add the onion and when the mixture comes to a boil, remove the onion and discard. Pour the milk into the cold roux, stirring continuously to avoid lumps. Simmer gently for two minutes. Add salt, ¼ teaspoon white pepper powder and a small pinch of nutmeg powder. Melt ½ tablespoon butter and layer the top of the sauce with it to avoid formation of skin.

TOMATO CONCASSE

Blanch 4 large tomatoes in boiling water for 2 minutes. Drain and cool slightly. Peel the tomatoes and halve them. Remove the seeds and chop the flesh roughly.

PAANCH PHORON

Mix together 1 tablespoon cumin seeds, ½ tablespoon fenugreek seeds, 1 tablespoon onion seeds, 1 tablespoon fennel seeds and 1 tablespoon mustard seeds.

GLOSSARY

English	Hindi
Almonds	Badam
Amaranth	Chouli/Chavli
Apple	Saeb
Asafoetida	Hing
Barley	Jau
Bay leaf	Tej patta
Beetroot	Chukandar
Bitter gourd	Karela
Black Bengal gram	Kale chane
Black cardamoms	Badi elaichi
Black grapes	Kale angoor
Black olives	Kala jaitun
Black pepper powder	Kali mirch powder
Black peppercorns	Kali mirch
Black salt	Kala namak
Black sesame seeds	Kale til
Boneless chicken	Murgh boti
Bottle gourd	Lauki/Ghia/Doodhi
Bread	Double roti
Brinjal	Baingan
Broken wheat	Dalia
Butter	Makkhan
Button mushrooms	Kukkurmutta/Dhingri
Cabbage	Pattagobhi
Carom seeds	Ajwain
Carrots	Gajar
Cashewnuts	Kaju
Caster sugar	Pisi hui chini
Cauliflower	Phoolgobhi
Celery	Ajmud
Chicken	Murgh
Chicken breasts	Murgh ka seena
Chicken legs	Murgh ki tangdi
Chickpeas	Kabuli chana
Cinnamon	Dalchini
Cinnamon powder	Dalchini powder
Clove powder	Lavang powder
Cloves	Lavang
Cluster beans	Guar
Coconut	Nariyal
Coconut milk	Nariyal ka doodh
Coriander powder	Dhania powder
Coriander seeds	Sabut dhania
Corn niblets/kernels	Makai ke dane
Cottage cheese	Paneer
Cucumber	Kakdi/Kheera
Cumin powder	Jeera powder
Cumin seeds	Jeera
Curry leaves	Kadi patta/ meetha neem
Dates	Khajur
Dill	Suva
Dried mango powder	Amchur
Dried pomegranate seeds	Anardana
Dried red chillies	Sookhi lal mirch
Edible silver foil	Chandi ka varq
Egg	Anda
Egg white	Ande ki safedi
Fennel seeds	Saunf
Fenugreek seeds	Methi dana
Fig	Anjeer
Flax seeds/Linseed	Alsi
French beans	Farsi
Fresh basil leaves	Tulsi ke patte
Fresh coriander leaves	Hara dhania
Fresh cream	Malai
Fresh fenugreek leaves	Methi
Fresh mint leaves	Pudina
Fresh spinach leaves	Palak
Garlic	Lehsun
Garlic paste	Lehsun ka paste
Ginger	Adrak
Ginger paste	Adrak ka paste
Gram flour	Besan
Green capsicum	Hari shimla mirch
Green cardamoms	Chhoti elaichi
Green chillies	Hari mirch
Green grapes	Hare angoor
Green olives	Hare jaitun
Green peas	Matar
Guavas	Amrud/Peru
Honey	Shahad/Madhu
Iceberg lettuce	Salad ke patte
Indian gooseberry	Amla

GLOSSARY

English	Hindi
Indian salmon	Rawas
Jaggery	Gur
Lemon juice	Nimboo ka ras
Lemon	Nimboo
Lemon zest	Nimboo ka chilka
Lettuce leaves	Salad ke patte
Mace	Javitri
Mackerel	Bangda
Mango pulp	Aam ka guda
Milk	Doodh
Millet	Bajra
Minced chicken	Murgh ka keema
Minced mutton	Keema
Mustard oil	Rai ka tel/ sarson ka tel
Mustard seeds	Rai/sarson
Oats	Jav
Oil	Tel
Olive oil	Jaitun ka tel
Onion seeds	Kalonji
Onions	Pyaaz
Orange	Narangi/Santra
Orange juice	Santre ka ras
Parboiled rice	Ukda chawal
Peanuts/ground nuts	Moongphali
Pinenuts	Chilgoza
Pistachio	Pista
Plums	Aloobukara
Pomfret	Halva/Saranga/ Chandwa/Poplait/ Machli
Poppy seeds	Khuskhus
Potatoes	Aloo
Powdered sugar	Pisi hui cheeni
Pure ghee	Desi ghee
Radish	Mooli
Raisins	Kishmish
Raw mangoes	Kachche aam
Raw peanuts	Kachchi Moongphali
Red capsicum	Lal Shimla Mirch
Red chilli flakes	Kooti hui sookhi lal mirch

English	Hindi
Red chilli powder	Lal mirch powder
Red grapes	Lal angoor
Red pumpkin	Kaddu
Refined flour	Maida
Rice	Chawal
Rice flour	Chawal ka atta
Ripe bananas	Pake kele
Roasted cumin powder	Bhuna jeera powder
Rock salt	Sendha namak
Saffron	Kesar
Salt	Namak
Screwpine essence	Kewra jal
Sea salt	Samudri namak
Semolina	Rawa/Suji
Sesame seeds	Til
Shallots	Chhote pyaaz
Sorrel leaves	Khatti bhaji
Sorghum	Jowar
Split Bengal gram	Chana dal
Split black gram skinless	Dhuli urad dal
Split green gram skinless	Dhuli moong dal
Split pigeon peas	Toovar dal/Arhar dal
Spinach	Palak
Spring onion	Hara pyaaz
Spring onion greens	Hare pyaaz ki patti
Sprouted green gram	Ankurit moong
Star anise	Phool chakri/Badiyan
Sugar	Cheeni/Shakkar
Sweet lime	Moosambi
Sweet potato	Shakkarkand/Rattalu
Tamarind	Imli
Tomatoes	Tamatar
Turmeric powder	Haldi powder
Unripe mango	Kachcha aam
Vinegar	Sirka
Walnut	Akhrot
Whole green gram	Sabut moong
Whole red lentils	Sabut masoor
Whole wheat flour	Atta
Yellow capsicum	Pili shimla mirch
Yogurt	Dahi
Zucchini	Tori/Turaii

MEASUREMENTS

Item	Quantity	Weight
Almonds	10	15 grams
Apple	1 medium	120 grams
Asafoetida (hing)	1 teaspoon	4 gms
Baby corn	10	125 grams
Bajra flour	1 cup	125 grams
Baking powder	1 teaspoon	3 grams
Baking soda (soda bicarbonate)	1 teaspoon	4 grams
Barley (jau)	1 cup	170 grams
Bay leaf	1	0.5 gram
Beetroot	1 medium	145 grams
Bitter gourd (karela)	1 medium	75 grams
Black cardamoms	11	10 grams
Black grapes	10	40 grams
Black pepper powder	1 teaspoon	3 grams
Black peppercorns	5	1 gram
Black salt	1 teaspoon	5 grams
Boneless skinless chicken breast	1	125 grams
Bottle gourd (lauki/doodhi)	1 medium	500 grams
Breadcrumbs	1 cup	110 grams
Brinjal (bharta)	1 large	650 grams
Brinjal, medium	1	30 grams
Broccoli, small florets	5	15 grams
Broken wheat	½ cup	100 grams
Brown bread	1 slice	30 grams
Brown sugar	1 cup	200 grams
Butter	1 tablespoon	15 grams
Butter	1 cup	150 grams
Button mushrooms	10 medium	125 grams
Cabbage	1 medium	650 grams
Carom seeds (ajwain)	1 teaspoon	2 grams
Carrot, grated	1 cup	150 grams
Carrot	1 medium	90 grams
Cashewnuts	10	20 grams
Castor sugar	1 cup	125 grams
Cauliflower	1 medium	500 grams
Chaat masala	1 teaspoon	1 gram
Chicken mince	½ cup	100 grams
Chickpeas	½ cup	100 grams
Chopped dates	1 cup	175 grams
Cinnamon	1 inch	0.5 gram
Cloves	10	1 gram
Coconut, freshly scraped	1 cup	110 grams
Coconut milk	1 cup	200 mls
Cooked rice (plain)	1 cup	150 grams
Coriander powder	1 teaspoon	2 grams

Item	Quantity	Weight
Coriander seeds	1 teaspoon	2 grams
Coriander seeds	1 tablespoon	6 grams
Corn kernels	1 cup	150 grams
Cornflour	1 tablespoon	5 grams
Cottage cheese (paneer), grated	½ cup	70 grams
Cucumber	1 medium	125 grams
Cumin powder	1 teaspoon	3 grams
Cumin seeds	1 tablespoon	9 grams
Curry leaves	10	1 gram
Dark chocolate chips	1 tablespoon	12 grams
Desiccated coconut	2 tablespoons	10 grams
Dried figs	¾ cup	900 grams
Dried fenugreek leaves (kasuri methi)	1 tablespoon	1 gram
Dried mango powder (amchur)	1 teaspoon	1 gram
Dried pomegranate seeds	1 teaspoon	3 grams
Dried red chillies	10	20 grams
Egg	1	50 grams
Fennel seeds (saunf)	1 teaspoon	3 grams
Fenugreek seeds (methi dana)	1 tablespoon	12 grams
Fenugreek seeds (methi dana)	1 teaspoon	5 grams
French beans	10	75 grams
Fresh button mushrooms	10 medium	125 grams
Fresh coriander leaves	1 medium bunch	250 grams
Fresh cream	1 cup	200 mls
Fresh cream	4 tablespoons	60 mls
Fresh fenugreek leaves	1 small bunch	175 grams
Fresh green peas, shelled	1 cup	150 grams
Fresh mint leaves	1 medium bunch	85 grams
Fresh pomegranate pearls	1 cup	180 grams
Fresh pomegranate pearls	1 tablespoon	10 grams
Fresh spinach leaves	1 small bunch	150 grams
Fresh spinach leaves	1 medium bunch	250 grams
Garam masala powder	1 teaspoon	2 grams
Garlic	10 cloves	15 grams
Garlic pasge	1 tablespoon	15 grams
Ginger	½ inch	5 grams
Ginger	1 inch piece	10 grams
Ginger paste	1 tablespoon	15 grams
Gram flour (besan)	1 cup	100 grams
Gram flour (besan)	1 tablespoon	5 grams
Grated cheese	1 cup	100 grams
Green capsicum	1 medium	110 grams
Green cardamom powder	1 teaspoon	2 grams
Green cardamoms	10	3 grams